THE EVERYTHING KIDS' EASY Science Experiments BOOK

Explore the world of science through
quick and fun experiments!

J. Elizabeth Mills

Adamsmedia
Avon, Massachusetts

PUBLISHER Karen Cooper

DIRECTOR OF ACQUISITIONS AND INNOVATION Paula Munier

MANAGING EDITOR, EVERYTHING° SERIES Lisa Laing

COPY CHIEF Casey Ebert

ACQUISITIONS EDITOR Katrina Schroeder

ASSOCIATE DEVELOPMENT EDITOR Hillary Thompson

SENIOR DEVELOPMENT EDITOR Brett Palana-Shanahan

EDITORIAL ASSISTANT Ross Weisman

EVERYTHING° SERIES COVER DESIGNER Erin Alexander

LAYOUT DESIGNERS Colleen Cunningham, Elisabeth Lariviere, Ashley Vierra, Denise Wallace

An Everything® Series Book.
Everything® and everything.com® are registered trademarks of F+W Media, Inc.

Published by Adams Media, a division of F+W Media, Inc.
57 Littlefield Street, Avon, MA 02322. U.S.A.
www.adamsmedia.com

ISBN 10: 1-4405-0158-0
ISBN 13: 978-1-4405-0158-6
eISBN 10: 1-4405-0159-9
eISBN 13: 978-1-4405-0159-3

Printed by RR Donnelley, Owensville, MO, US

10 9 8 7 6 5 4 3 2 1

February 2010

This publication is designed to provide accurate and authoritative information with regard to the subject matter covered. It is sold with the understanding that the publisher is not engaged in rendering legal, accounting, or other professional advice. If legal advice or other expert assistance is required, the services of a competent professional person should be sought.
—From a *Declaration of Principles* jointly adopted by a Committee of the American Bar Association and a Committee of Publishers and Associations

Many of the designations used by manufacturers and sellers to distinguish their products are claimed as trademarks. When those designations appear in this book and Adams Media was aware of a trademark claim, the designations have been printed with initial capital letters.

Interior illustrations by Kurt Dolber.
Puzzles by Beth L. Blair.

This book is available at quantity discounts for bulk purchases.
For information, please call 1-800-289-0963.

Visit the entire Everything® series at *www.everything.com*

To Andrew, whose curiosity knows no bounds
and who always inspires me to learn more.

Acknowledgments

My deepest thanks to the scientists in my life: Andrew, Eugene, Agnieszka, Fabrice, Costa, Fred, and my brother Michael. I owe you all so much homemade guacamole!

And thank you to my agent, Gina Panettieri, for this incredible project, and thanks for all your invaluable input and experiment ideas. We have a great partnership!

Contents

Introduction

Things are always happening all around us—dark clouds building in a clear blue sky, leaves changing from bright green to gold and crimson, smoke filling the air we breathe, and our planet rotating around the sun.

What's going on? Who is affected? When will these things happen again? Why do they happen at all? Scientists ask questions like these to help them understand Earth's incredible forces and transformations. You can be a scientist, too, and find answers to all kinds of questions.

But scientists are grownups, you think, with tools like microscopes and test tubes, and they know more than you do. In fact, scientists all start out with a sense of curiosity. That's the first, and most important, tool you will need. And one you already have. Every time you ask why, every time you wonder whether something will happen the same way if you try doing it a different way, you're building your curiosity. You're becoming a scientist.

Science is about observing, doing, and learning. Sometimes in science experiments you make things bubble and boil, sometimes things even explode! But other times you are watching something change very slowly. Or you are watching animals outside to learn where they live and what they eat. During an experiment, a scientist writes down what she sees, smells, hears, feels, and sometimes what she tastes. Then she looks at her notes and tries to understand what she has just observed.

Cool Quotes

Every individual matters. Every individual has a role to play. Every individual makes a difference.

—Jane Goodall

This book will take you through the five main areas of science—biology, chemistry, physics, the human body, and planet Earth. The experiments you can do on your own or with a friend are called Try This. The experiments that require help from a grownup are called Science Labs. These sometimes involve a knife or a stove. It's important to be safe when you're a scientist.

The experiments are set in a certain order, but you can always flip through and pick an experiment you like. These activities are meant to be relatively easy to set up, do, and take down. However, if you think of ways to extend the fun, go for it. You might just discover something completely new!

Nature

The world around us is full of so many living things that we are always trying to better understand. Scientists go out in the world and watch to see how plants grow, where animals make their homes, what insects eat, and more so they can learn more about the natural world. In the following experiments, you will be going for walks in your neighborhood and backyard to observe and learn.

TRY THIS
LEAF HUNT

Whether it's fall, winter, spring, or summer, there are usually leaves—blowing about in the wind, crunching under your feet, adding colors to a gray sidewalk. They grow on broad, towering elms and oaks and on tiny, wispy Japanese maples. What do these leaves do? Why are they attached to trees? What happens when the leaves fall and why do they change color? How do trees grow new leaves? All these questions can be answered by looking more closely at leaves and the trees to which they belong.

QUESTION

What kinds of leaves are in your neighborhood?

Why did the leaf go to see the doctor?

It was feeling green!

WHAT YOU NEED

Shoes
Bag
Magnifying Glass
Paper
Crayons

WHAT TO DO

1. Put on your shoes. You're going on a nature hike!
2. Look all around you as you walk. Pick up leaves you see on the ground and put them in your bag. When you think you have enough different leaves, head back home.
3. Lay out your leaves on a table. Sort them into piles by their shape. How many of each kind of leaf do you have?
4. Use your magnifying glass to look at the leaves up close. What do you see?
5. Put a piece of paper on top of your favorite leaf. Carefully rub a crayon over the area of the paper that covers the leaf. What do you notice about your picture?

WHAT'S HAPPENING

A tree is made up of a main trunk, branches that grow from the trunk, leaves that grow from the branches, and a root system underground that helps keep the tree upright and healthy.

Different trees have differently shaped leaves. Some leaves are pointy, some are round. Trees that lose their leaves in the fall are called *deciduous* trees. They grow new leaves in the spring. These leaves soak in sunlight and turn it into energy for the tree. The leaf stems carry food from the leaves to the trunk and the rest of the tree. Deciduous trees include elms, oaks, maples, and others. Trees that do not lose their leaves are called *coniferous*—their "leaves" are pine needles. Pines, firs, and spruces are coniferous trees.

WORDS to KNOW

deciduous: trees that shed their leaves in fall and grow new ones in spring.

coniferous: evergreen trees and shrubs that have needles instead of leaves.

YOUR NOTES

You can save your leaves for a later experiment. Or you can use them to make natural "stained glass." Press your leaves between the pages of a book. After a couple days, when the leaves are flat and dry, arrange them on a sheet of wax paper. Place another piece of wax paper on top. Ask a grownup to run an iron over the papers. Wait until the sheets are cool. Then use some string to hang your "stained glass" leaf artwork in the window!

TRY THIS
SUPER PINE CONES

Forests, parks, and neighborhood streets are full of old and young trees. How did the young trees begin? Trees make seeds that grow into saplings. The saplings then grow into trees. Some seeds are fruit—such as apples or cherries. Other seeds are nuts, such as acorns and chestnuts.

But seeds face many dangers. Animals like to eat fruit and nuts. And high winds and heavy rain can make seeds go bad or fall off the tree too soon. So trees have evolved clever ways to keep their seeds safe from hungry animals and bad weather so that the seeds can eventually find good soil and grow. For example, chestnuts have husks around them that break open when the chestnut fruit is ripe and falls from the tree.

QUESTION

How do pine trees protect their seeds from bad weather?

WHAT YOU NEED

Dry pinecones
Large bowl
Water
Paper towel
Hair dryer

FUN FACT

Seed Snacks

Did you know that seeds can be great snacks? Pumpkins, squash, sunflowers, and sesame plants all have seeds that taste yummy, especially when you toast them in the oven. You can mix them with raisins and chocolate for a perfect trail mix.

FUN FACT

Super Cones

The Sugar pine tree produces the longest cones in the world. Some cones can be up to 2 feet long!

WHAT TO DO

1. Find some pinecones outside or at the store.
2. Put the cones in a bowl. Cover them with water.
3. Now watch! What happens to the pinecones?
4. Take the cones out and put them on a paper towel to dry.
5. Use a hair dryer to help the cones dry faster. What happens?

WHAT'S HAPPENING

A pine tree hides its seeds in cones—a shell that can expand and contract with water. When the cone gets wet, the shell shrinks, keeping the inner seeds nice and dry. Then when the cone dries, the shell expands, opening up to let the wind blow the seeds away so they can grow somewhere else.

Some scientists believe that pinecones can play a role in forecasting the weather. This is because cones open and close depending on the humidity in the air. If a cone is open, the air must be dry so the upcoming weather could stay dry. But if a cone is closed, then there's already moisture in the air and the upcoming weather could bring rain. Look at some pinecones near where you live. Are they open or closed? What is the weather outside? Are the pinecones accurate in their forecast?

FUN FACT

Johnny Appleseed

There once was a man who planted apple trees all over the Midwest in the late 1700s. His nickname was Johnny Appleseed, but his real name was John Chapman. He was born on September 26, 1774.

Cool Quotes

We must believe that we are gifted for something, and that this thing, at whatever cost, must be attained.

—Marie Curie

seed: a grain or fruit that enables a plant to reproduce itself.

YOUR NOTES

Draw a picture of your pinecones, first when they're dry and then when they're wet.

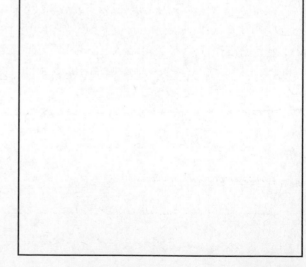

Bubbles and Butter

Almost every day we eat something that a teeny tiny organism helps to make. To learn something about this little critter, solve the Falling Letter puzzle below. Figure out where to put the letters in each column. The letters all fit in the boxes under their own column, but not always in the same order! The black boxes are the spaces between words.

How do I butter this?

It's easier _after_ you bake it!

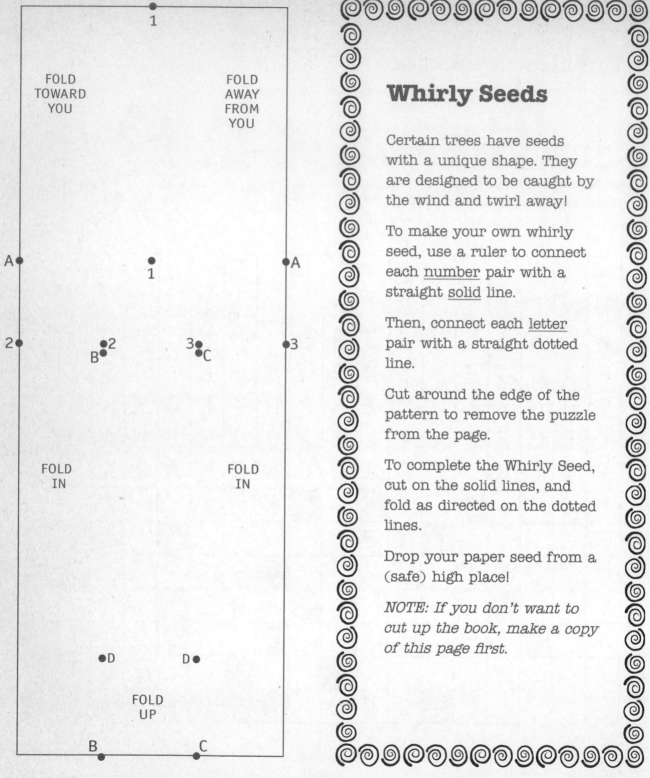

FOLD
TOWARD
YOU

FOLD
AWAY
FROM
YOU

1

A

1

A

2

B 2

3 C

3

FOLD
IN

FOLD
IN

D

D

FOLD
UP

B

C

Whirly Seeds

Certain trees have seeds with a unique shape. They are designed to be caught by the wind and twirl away!

To make your own whirly seed, use a ruler to connect each <u>number</u> pair with a straight <u>solid</u> line.

Then, connect each <u>letter</u> pair with a straight dotted line.

Cut around the edge of the pattern to remove the puzzle from the page.

To complete the Whirly Seed, cut on the solid lines, and fold as directed on the dotted lines.

Drop your paper seed from a (safe) high place!

NOTE: If you don't want to cut up the book, make a copy of this page first.

SCIENCE LAB:
SOCKS, SEEDS, AND APPLES

If too many seeds grow in the same place, the new plants have to compete for resources, such as sunlight and water and nutrients in the soil. So it's a good thing for seeds to travel to new locations where it's not so crowded. That way, the seeds can find the perfect soil in which to grow and thrive.

QUESTION

How do seeds travel?

WHAT YOU NEED

Old socks (they're going to get dirty, so
    don't pick new ones)
Sunny day
Cellophane tape
Piece of paper
Apple
Knife
Adult

WHAT TO DO

1. Put on your socks and go out to your backyard.
2. Now go back inside and take off your socks. What do you see?
3. Use the cellophane tape to take off any seeds from your socks.
4. Place the tape on a piece of paper so you can look at the seeds. Do you recognize any of them?
5. Now ask an adult to cut open an apple lengthwise. What do you see inside?

WHAT'S HAPPENING

Seeds travel many different ways. Sometimes plants get help from animals such as squirrels, who bury nuts in all kinds of places, and light breezes that blow dandelion seeds into the air.

**How do you know if a
tree is a dogwood?**

By its bark!

Flowers make seeds, too, in the form of pollen. And bees help make new flowers by carrying pollen from one blossom to the next. When a bee lands on a flower, it drinks some nectar. The bee will later turn the nectar into honey. But first, the bee picks up some pollen powder on its legs. When the bee visits another flower, it leaves some of the powder behind. This powder helps the second flower make its own pollen, which results in more flowers. Flowers need bees and bees need flowers.

Fruit trees hide their seeds inside tasty treats. Apple seeds grow into trees that make flowers that turn into fruit. When animals eat the fruits, they also eat the seeds. So the seeds travel inside the animals and pass into the soil through the animals' droppings. Be careful not to step in any droppings outside!

YOUR NOTES

Try going out in your socks at different times of the day and during different times of the year. Do you find new seeds on your socks?

Try cutting open other fruits. Which ones have seeds?

Criss-Cross

Some biologists experiment with combining plants or animals with different characteristics to get new plants or animals that are better. Break the First to Last, Letter Shift, and Vowel Scramble codes to see if you think this silly scientist was successful with his crazy experiment!

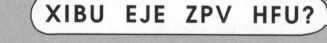

I ROSSEDC A OGD ITHW A OOMERANGB.

XIBU EJE ZPV HFU?

U PAT THUT RONS UWUY, BOT ULWUYS CIMAS BUCK!

Ecosystems

Our world is a collection of all kinds of *ecosystems*. An ecosystem is a community of animals, plants, trees, insects, their habitats, and the climate in which they live. Everyone in these communities shares food and natural resources. Ecosystems can be as big as the whole world and as tiny as a rock.

A tree is a great example of an ecosystem. It provides a habitat for squirrels, birds, and insects. It provides shade for plants on the ground. It drinks in sunlight to grow bigger and make seeds that the squirrels and birds eat and scatter around. Birds also eat the insects. And when the tree dies, it becomes a part of the ground again, helping the new trees grow big and strong.

WORDS to KNOW

community: a group that interacts and lives in a common area.

ecosystem: a community of living things.

TRY THIS
FRIENDLY NEIGHBORS

Because members of a community share resources and rely on each other, it's important to know your neighbors. That way, you can all work together to solve problems and look out for each other in hard times.

QUESTION

Who lives in your community?

WHAT YOU NEED

Pencil
Paper
Shoes

Going Buggy!

Insects are the largest animal group on earth. There may be as many as 750,000 different insect species!

WHAT TO DO

1. Put on your shoes—you're going on a neighbor walk!
2. Who do you see in your neighborhood? Write down the animals, bugs, and people you see. These are the members of your community.
3. Count how many you see of the same kind of neighbor. What did you find out?

WHAT'S HAPPENING

Think about how your life impacts the lives of your neighbors, both animal and human. If the resources in an ecosystem are harmed, if the water becomes polluted, or an animal species is removed, the whole ecosystem is hurt. It's important to see ourselves as part of a larger web of life. What we do matters in so many ways.

YOUR NOTES

Now that you know who is in your community, think about what resources all of you share. Do you share city utilities like water and electricity? Do you share food and weather? How can we take better care of our community?

TRY THIS
HOME SWEET HOME

What does your home look like? Is it big or small? Is it made of wood or bricks? Who lives in your house? Living things live in all kinds of homes, made of all kinds of materials. Sometimes these houses are high up in a tree, or underwater in a lake, or deep underground in the soil. Where would you build your house if you could live anywhere in the natural world?

QUESTION

Where do the members of your community live?

WHAT YOU NEED

Shoes
Pencil
Paper

WHAT TO DO

1. Go for a walk around your backyard. Keep a lookout for any kind of creature—bug, bird, or animal.
2. Where are the birds flying to? Where are the bugs crawling or flying to? Where do people go at the end of the day? Write these places down on your paper.
3. Now head home and look at your list. Do any places have more than one resident? Do birds and squirrels live in the same places? Do spiders and people live in the same places? Can you add more details to your list to give these roommates their own homes?

WHAT'S HAPPENING

Ecosystems are made up of *habitats*—places where the members of the community live. These places may be natural, like trees and holes in the ground, or man-made, like houses. Natural habitats keep birds, animals, and/or insects safe and dry. And they also provide safe places for animal mothers to have babies and raise them.

Hidden Habitat

Look closely at this kid's messy habitat. Can you find the mushroom, mouse, spider, snake, lizard, owl, crow, sunflower, dragonfly, and snail?

WORDS to KNOW

habitat: the place where a plant or an animal usually lives and gets what it needs to live.

Ecosystems are also referred to as *biomes*. The major biomes are deserts, grasslands, tundra, forests, and freshwater and saltwater environments. These environments consist of specific animals and plants, and climates that are specific to each biome.

YOUR NOTES

Draw a picture of the habitat you found with the most inhabitants.

SCIENCE LAB:
WHAT'S FOR DINNER?

All living things in an ecosystem are called *organisms*, and organisms are connected by food chains. Organisms need energy to live, and each living thing gets its energy from another part of the food chain.

Producers are the first link in the chain because they produce, or make, the resources used by other members of the food chain. Plants are producers. They turn sunlight into sugar and oxygen that other living things use for energy. Consumers consume, or eat, producers. Certain animals, called *herbivores*, eat plants to get energy. Other animals, called *carnivores*, eat herbivores. They get energy from eating other animals. When producers and consumers die, the last link in the food chain takes over. That link is the decomposers. They break down the animals and plants so that they can nourish the next generation.

QUESTION

What parts of your food chain do you eat? Where are you on the food chain?

WHAT YOU NEED

Paper
Pencil
Fridge

WHAT TO DO

1. Using paper and pencil, make a list of everything you ate in your last meal. If you can't remember, open your fridge and take a look at its contents.

2. Draw a square around the foods that came from plants. These could be lettuce, spinach, or fresh herbs like rosemary or basil. Fruits and vegetables like tomatoes, cucumbers, pumpkins, strawberries, and peppers all come from plants.

3. Draw a circle around foods that came from animals. These could be sausage, ham, beef, pork, chicken, cheese, or eggs.

4. Draw a triangle around all the liquids, like milk and juice.

5. Draw a star around all the solids.

6. Take a look at your list. What do you see? Do any foods have multiple shapes around them?

WHAT'S HAPPENING

Humans are *omnivores*, which means we eat plants and animals. And we are at the top of the food chain. If we pollute the waters, litter the land, or consume too much, we harm the delicate balance in the food chain.

Food chains often overlap. Animals will eat different kinds of food to survive, and sometimes that food is a part of a separate food chain. If you draw lines between the organisms in multiple food chains according to who eats whom, you create a food web. Food webs are often complex, and they show how animals and plants are affected by changes in their habitats. The rainforests hold more than half of all the animal and plant species in the world. So there are millions of food chains in the rainforest biome.

WORDS to KNOW

herbivore: animal that eats only plants.

carnivore: animal that eats other animals.

YOUR NOTES

Even though humans are omnivores, some of us eat more plants or more animals. What do you like to eat? Are you more of an herbivore or more of a carnivore?

Who in your family is a producer? Who is a consumer?

What is a plumber's favorite vegetable?

A leek!

Diamond Poem

A diamante is a type of poem shaped like a diamond. It is used to combine thoughts about two different elements, such as a bird and a fish. To create a diamante about ecosystems, use the words around the edge of the page to fill in the pattern.

DESERT

WAVING

OCEAN

HOT

CRASHING

LIZARD

BLOWING

DRY

SPRAYING

SALTY

_____
One noun that is contrasting to line 7

_____
Two adjectives that describe line 1

_____
Three action verbs ending in -ing that describe line 1

_____
Four nouns *(First 2 nouns relate to line 1, Last 2 nouns relate to line 7)*

_____
Three action verbs ending in -ing that describe line 7

WET

_____
Two adjectives that describe line 7

BAKING

SAND

SAMPLE:
bird
loud, feathered
flying, chirping, pecking
robin, sparrow, beta, trout
swimming, diving, wiggling
quiet, scaly
fish

_____
One noun that is contrasting to line 1

DRIFTING

BOAT

FISH

Food Chain

A food chain goes from small to big—the most simple plants and animals are used as food by the next bigger organism. Unscramble the words at the bottom of the puzzle. Can you put together two different food chains?

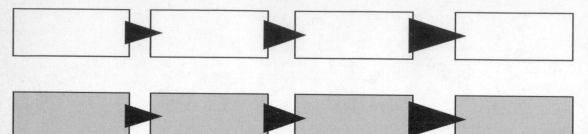

rasgs   nasil   isfh   rasgsoppher   atr   easugll   naske   easeewd

Classification

Scientists have found that certain kinds of animals share the same traits—the same kind of food, the same habitat, the same call. The more traits these animals have in common, the more likely they are to share the same classification.

Big groupings, with lots of animals and plants in them, are called kingdoms. The two main kingdoms are the animal kingdom and the plant kingdom. As scientists start finding fewer things in common, these kingdoms get smaller and become groups. The two main groups in the animal kingdom are vertebrates—animals that have a spine—and invertebrates —animals that don't have a spine. The main groups in the plant kingdom are flowering plants and nonflowering plants. These divisions help scientists better understand our natural world.

TRY THIS
BIG, SMALL, NESTS FOR ALL

Have you ever looked up into a tree and seen a bird's nest? It's an amazing feat of construction, built with simple materials using only a beak. They sometimes use things like twigs, leaves, and grass, and even string, bits of cloth, or strands of hair.

QUESTION

How do birds build little nests and big nests?

WHAT YOU NEED

For the little nest:
Small twigs from outside
Glue
String
Cotton balls
Leaves from earlier experiment

For the big nest:
Blankets
Pillows
Sheets

WHAT TO DO

Little Nest
1. With the help of a grownup, place sticks in a circle, gluing the overlapping ends together.
2. Add another layer of sticks and glue. You can insert bits of string, cotton, and leaves to soften the nest.
3. Keep adding layers until you have a cup-shaped nest.

FUN FACT

Home Beak Home

Birds are born knowing how to make the right nest for their species. But they do need to practice. Birds get better at building nests the more they build them!

Nest Names

Did you know nests have names? A badger's nest is called a sett. A wasps' nest is called a vespiary. A hare's nest is called a hide. And an eagle's nest is called an eyrie.

4. If you like, you can place your nest in a low tree and watch to see if any birds adopt it.

Big Nest

1. Lay one blanket on the floor. This is the base of your nest.
2. Take a second blanket and roll it up on the floor. Fold the roll into a triangle and place it on top of the first blanket.
3. Take another blanket and do the same thing. But when you place it on top of the second blanket, turn it to the right a little bit so that the points don't line up.
4. Do the same with two or three more blankets or sheets.
5. Now grab a couple pillows and get in. Ready for bed?

WHAT'S HAPPENING

Birds' nests are a common kind of habitat in an ecosystem. Birds make nests to lay eggs in and to raise their young. Some build their nests in trees; others build them on the ground or even in water. Eagles put their nests on rocky ledges. There are birds that don't make nests at all. They use other birds' nests. A father Emperor penguin nestles his egg up against his warm body to keep the egg safe and dry. There are insects and animals that make nests, too. Wasps construct them high up in attics and trees and other sheltered spots. And squirrels make nests, as do some fish, reptiles, termites, and others. Each species wants to protect its babies so they will grow and continue the species.

YOUR NOTES

Was it easy to build these nests with your hands? Try building the large nest with only your feet. Can you imagine putting a nest together with only a beak?

TRY THIS
WACKY WALKS

Go for a walk across the room. Break into a run. Hop, skip, and jump. We all move in different ways. So do animals, insects, and birds. Their bodies are shaped in certain ways that allow them to walk and run the way they do. How an animal moves is called its gait.

In this experiment, you're going to try out several animals' gaits to learn how they move. Who knows, maybe you'll find a new way to groove!

QUESTION

Why do animals walk the way they do?

WHAT YOU NEED

Imagination
Lots of open space

WHAT TO DO

1. Some birds don't fly; they walk. But their walks can look pretty funny. Try waddling like a penguin.
2. Giraffes have long legs and long necks. Try getting on all fours and sticking your neck out. Now try taking long strides.
3. In the ocean, animals move very differently than they do on land. A whale swishes his big tail from side to side to move through the water. Lie on your stomach on the floor with your arms at your sides. Now try swishing your feet from side to side. Can you move across the floor?
4. Rabbits and frogs hop about. They push off of their strong back legs and spring into the air. Make sure you have

FUN FACT

Zoom!

Cheetahs are the fastest animals on land. They can run at over 62 miles per hour—three times as fast as the fastest human runner.

WORDS to KNOW

gait: how an animal moves.

plenty of space, then try hopping around the room. How far can you go?

5. Humans walk upright on their legs and swing their arms to help them move. Walk around the room, swinging your arms.

6. Some animals, like cats and dogs, walk on their toes. This allows them to move quietly and chase prey. Try walking on your toes as silently as you can. Did anyone hear you coming?

7. Rhinos, and other big mammals, are big and lumbering. They make a lot of noise as they walk. Try stomping around as loud as you can.

WHAT'S HAPPENING

Each animal has developed its own way of moving. Birds use their wings to fly; rabbits use their strong hind legs to hop; giraffes use their long legs to stride gracefully across the open plains.

These gaits can also help in case of danger. Birds can fly into the air if they are threatened on the ground. Penguins don't move very fast on land, but they can dive into the water where they are speedy swimmers. Rabbits can hop away very fast. Giraffes can see danger coming from far off, and their strides are so long that they are hard to catch.

Each gait is suited to that particular animal, too. A rabbit would have trouble walking like a giraffe, and a frog would have trouble swimming like a whale. You have special bones in your legs and feet that help you walk the way you do. So you are built just the way you are supposed to walk. But it's fun to pretend!

Snake in a Tree

If you want to find a rat snake, you may have to look up—in a tree! Rat snakes climb trees to find birds and eggs to eat. Their bodies are specially made to slither up bark.

YOUR NOTES

What was the easiest way for you to move about? What was your favorite way to move? Can you think of other animals whose gaits you could imitate? How about a crab or a snake?

SCIENCE LAB:
A GAGGLE OF GEESE

Sorting and classifying are two of the most basic skills everyone learns. Do you put all your toys in one place in your room and your clothes in another place? Do you put your pencils in one section of your backpack and your books in another? This skill helps you to keep order in your world—to understand where things are and what is similar and different about those things. Scientists go through the same process when they observe the natural world. And once they're done sorting, scientists then give names to the groupings they've created.

QUESTION

How do scientists group the animals and plants in our world?

WHAT YOU NEED

Data from the previous experiments
Paper
Pencil

WHAT TO DO

1. For each experiment, look at the data you've gathered.
2. For the leaf experiment, think of ways you can group the leaves you found. Big/small? Pointy/round? Green/yellow? Maple/oak?
3. For the seed experiments, how can you group the seeds? Big/small? Shell/husk? Edible/nonedible? Flying/falling?
4. For the community experiment, how can you group your neighbors? Big/small? Insects/animals/people? Flying/crawling/walking? Fur/feathers/skin? Color?
5. For the habitat experiment, how can you group the habitats? Tree/ground? Hole/nest/house? Brick/twigs/stone?
6. For the food chain experiment, how can you group the foods? Sweet/sour/salty? Breakfast/lunch/dinner? Old/new? Liquid/solid? Vegetable/fruit? Meat/dairy?
7. For the walking experiment, how can you group the animals by their movement? Hoppers? Striders? Swimmers? Flyers?

8. Now find ways to narrow your groups. You're revising your research to be as specific and detailed as you can. This is what scientists do.

WHAT'S HAPPENING

Scientists have formal ways that they classify animals, plants, insects, and so on. They look for a grouping, say all the yellow flowers in a garden. Then they look to see what those yellow-flowered plants have in common and what their differences are. Based on those conclusions, scientists group the plants under one classification or another.

You, however, can classify animals and plants and other things any way you like. But you want your classifications to help you better understand your world. So you should make sure that your group names refer to the way an animal walks, what an insect eats, where a plant grows, and so on. Sorting and classifying are very important to scientists.

YOUR NOTES

How would you classify yourself using the groups above?

_____

_____

_____

_____

_____

_____

_____

_____

_____

_____

_____

_____

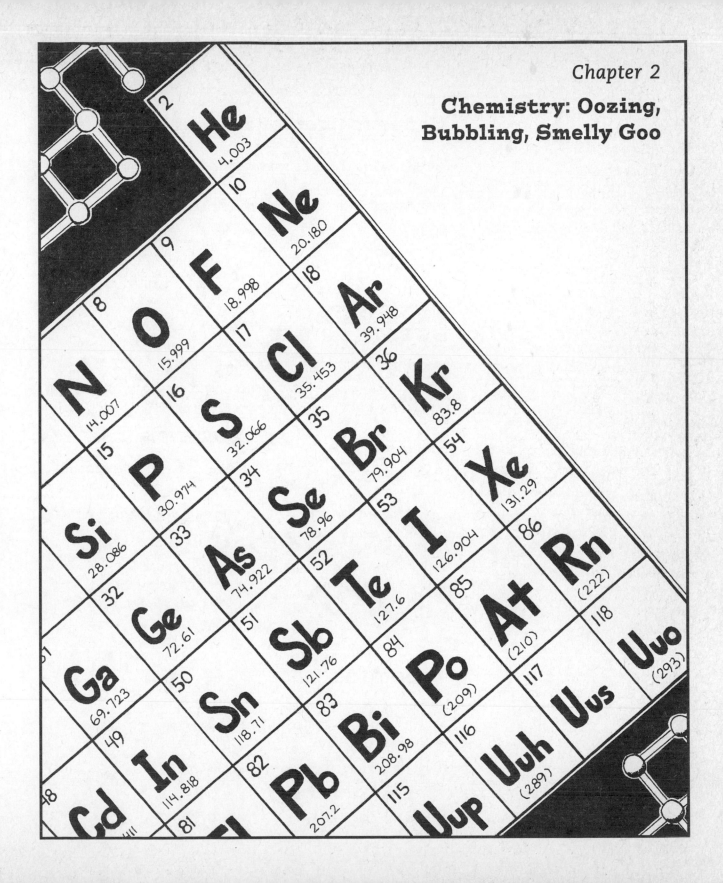

Chapter 2

Chemistry: Oozing, Bubbling, Smelly Goo

Condensation and Freezing

Clouds gather on a stormy day, dew catches on a spider web, snowflakes fall, and ice cracks. Water takes on many forms in the world around us. It turns to vapor and forms droplets that make the clouds that rain down and moisturize the earth. And water freezes and turns to snow and ice. How does this happen?

TRY THIS
SWEATY SODAS!

If you hold a cold glass of water on a hot day, the glass gets sweaty. That moisture is called condensation.

QUESTION

What causes condensation?

WHAT YOU NEED

2 plastic cups
Water
Ice
Towel
Stopwatch

WHAT TO DO

1. Fill one cup with water, almost to the top
2. Fill the other cup with ice. Then add water. The water should cover the ice.
3. Wipe off the outside of each cup with the towel to make sure both cups are dry.

4. Start your stopwatch. After fifteen minutes, check each cup.

WHAT'S HAPPENING

The outside of the cup with water is dry. But the outside of the cup with ice and water is wet. Congratulations, you've just made dew! If you've ever walked around in the wet grass on a cool summer morning, you've felt dew. The next time you take a hot bath or shower, look at the mirror when you get out of the tub. Why is it all fogged up?

The air around us is *saturated*, which means it is full of water vapor. Water vapor is the gas state of water. When you added ice to the second cup, the cup became cool. The cup then cooled the air around it. Cool air can't hold as much water vapor as warm air, so the water vapor becomes droplets of liquid. The drops attach to the cup. These drops are called dew. In the case of the mirror, the tiny drops of water from the steamy bath are clinging to the cold glass of the mirror. Draw a smiley face!

Later in this book you'll learn about meteorologists—people who study the weather. They use the dew point to tell the humidity of the air. Airline pilots also rely on dew point to fly safely in icy or foggy conditions.

YOUR NOTES

Try this experiment using fewer ice cubes. Is the outside of the cup less wet? Add more ice cubes and see what happens.

What if you use different kinds of containers, such as metal or glass?

Try this experiment in the bathroom after a hot steamy shower. What happens?

FUN FACT

Icy Breath

Did you know you can see water vapor? On a cold day, when you breathe out, you can see a white cloud. That cloud is condensed water vapor.

WORDS to KNOW

condensation: the process by which water changes from a gas to a liquid.

water vapor: water in the form of a gas, present in the atmosphere.

Do the experiment again, but put a thermometer in the cup with the ice. When you see dew appear, look at the temperature on the thermometer. This is the dew point temperature.

Record the time it takes dew to appear on the following lines.

Fewer ice cubes _____

More ice cubes _____

Metal container _____

Glass container _____

Steamy room _____

Dew point temperature _____

TRY THIS
JACK FROST'S SECRET

Have you ever seen icy patterns on your windows in the dead of winter? Where did they come from?

QUESTION

What causes frost?

WHAT YOU NEED

2 plastic cups

¼-cup measure

Rock salt (you can use the kind that's meant for making ice cream)

Ice

Water

Towel

WHAT TO DO

1. Fill one plastic cup so that it's half full of water.
2. Use the towel to wipe the outside of the cup to make sure it's dry.
3. Fill the cup with ice.
4. To the second cup, add ¼ cup water and ¼ cup rock salt.
5. Wipe that cup as well, and fill it with ice.
6. Now count to 15. Hold the water cup with one hand and scratch the outside with a fingernail. Do you notice anything?
7. Do the same with the cup that has the rock salt in it. What happens?
8. Keep scratching on the cup every 15 seconds or so. What kind of patterns can you make on your cup?

frost: the layer of tiny ice crystals on a cold surface.

WHAT'S HAPPENING

As you can see, a thin layer of white ice has formed on the outside of the cup with the rock salt. This is frost.

When you made dew in the last experiment, the water vapor cooled from a gas to a liquid. The rock salt in this experiment allowed the temperature of the water in the cup to get even colder, dipping below the dew point temperature. So now instead of drops of liquid on the outside of the glass with rock salt, you have ice crystals, or frost.

Outdoors, frost can cause problems. Car windows become coated in a hard white layer that's difficult to remove and impossible to see through. Flowers and fruits in gardens freeze, ending their growth period. But in the mountains, a special kind of ice crystals called hoar

Air-mazing

Air reacts with natural chemicals in some kinds of fruit. The result of this chemical reaction is very easy to see! Break the Upside-Down-Flip-Flop code for directions to do a colorful experiment that shows this reaction.

> ᶠˡᵒwᵉʳ ᵖˡᵒᵐⁿ'
> ᵐⁱˡˡ ᵖᵃᵛᵉ
> ᵃᵖᵖˡᵉ ˢˡⁱᶜᵉ
> ᵐᵒˡᵉ' ᵗʰᵉ
> ᵖᵒᵘˡ ᵒᶠ
> ᵃᵗᶠᵉˡ ᵃⁿ
> ᶜʰᵉᶜᵏ ⁱᶠ
> ⁱᶠ ᵐᵘᶜᵒᵛᵉˡᵉᵈ'
> ᵃᵖᵖˡᵉ' ˡᵉᵃᵛᵉ
> ˢˡⁱᶜᵉ ᵃⁿ

frost can cause a very big problem. If hoar frost forms on top of a layer of snow, and then the frost is covered by a new layer of snow, this can cause an avalanche. It's important to know what the weather is like when you go out in winter so you can be safe.

YOUR NOTES

You can test frost the same way you tested dew in the last experiment. Try different containers. Put the glass in the freezer. Does the frost appear more quickly? At what temperature does the frost appear? On the following lines, record the time it takes frost to appear.

Metal container _____
Glass container _____
Freezer _____
Frost point temperature _____

Cool Quotes

Science does not know its debt to imagination.

—Ralph Waldo Emerson

From the Piggy Bank

You can brew up a nice batch of copper acetate using a simple chemical reaction. To find directions on how to do this, you must choose between the two sets of different letters in the puzzle grid. Use a light-colored marker to highlight the set of letters you want, then read them from left to right, top to bottom.

S	i	O	f	A	y	K	o	A	u	F	a	O
r	L	D	e	E	r	D	e	P	A	a	P	d
E	i	R	n	T	O	g	W	E	t	L	h	i
s	I	s	N	e	t	V	I	N	o	E	f	l
G	A	e	R	.	t	L	A	t	Y	e	r	3
s	S	H	,	I	N	y	Y	o	u	N	E	w
W	i	P	E	l	N	N	l	I	E	g	S	e
t	O	t	h	N	e	T	O	w	P	.	r	W
o	A	n	I	T	g	a	2	n	4	s	w	e
r	H	O	t	U	R	o	S	.	t	T	H	h
E	i	G	R	s	E	E	p	N	u	C	z	O
L	O	R	z	Y	O	l	U	e	S	.	E	E
s	I	S	t	C	a	O	r	P	P	t	E	o
R	v	A	C	e	E	r	T	A	T	!	E	!

flavor must last a long time	must fizz when mixed with water	must feel good to chew	must not melt on your hands
must be extra crunchy .	**YUM-istry** Chemists work closely with candy makers to come up with the formulas for some of our favorite treats. Their job is to make sure each candy behaves the way it is supposed to. Which candy is described on this page? Cross out the box marked with a dot. Continue clockwise around the border crossing out every other box. Read the descriptions that remain.		must get soft but not gooey
must make good-sized bubbles			must pour easily
should be more sweet than salty	must not stick to the wrapper	must not form bubbles	must not dry out in the package

SCIENCE LAB:
SLIPPING, SLIDING AWAY!

Be careful walking outside in winter—there's often ice on the sidewalks. Walk slowly, make sure you can keep your balance, and then try sliding slowly along the ice. The slippery surface of ice allows you to slide over something that isn't usually slippery, like cement. But ice is dangerous and you can fall and hurt yourself. So towns usually try to keep their citizens safe by placing salt or sand on top of the ice to provide traction.

QUESTION

Which substance makes an icy surface less slippery: salt or sand?

WHAT YOU NEED

3 ice cubes
3 small plates
½-teaspoon measure
Salt
Sand
Stopwatch

WHAT TO DO

1. Place one ice cube on each plate.
2. Using the ½-teaspoon measure, add salt to the first cube and sand to the second cube. Leave the third cube alone.
3. Wait ten minutes. Then rub your finger over each cube. Which cube is melting the fastest? Which cube is not so slippery? Which cube is your control?

WHAT'S HAPPENING

As you discovered in the frost experiment, salt allows water to remain liquid at a lower temperature. So salt is the best way to melt icy sidewalks. But sand provides traction, which means your finger doesn't slide easily across the sandy cube. So if you want to walk safely across a slippery sidewalk, sand is the best thing to use. Also, the kind of salt that is used to melt ice outdoors is not good for the environment. So some cities are now using sand on wintry roads and sidewalks.

YOUR NOTES

Does your family use salt or sand outdoors in the winter? Try using sand instead of salt and see if you can walk more easily on the ice. Always walk carefully and hold an adult's hand if you think you might fall.

carbon dioxide: a colorless, odorless gas that is found in carbonated sodas.

FUN FACT

Raisin' a Raisin

Do you know how raisins are made? At the end of the summer, grapes are set out to dry in the sun. After a few weeks, the sun-dried grapes have turned into raisins.

What did one raisin say to the other raisin at the gym?

You're in "grape" shape!

Carbon Dioxide

Take a deep breath. Now let it out. You've just exhaled carbon dioxide, a gas that is used for so many things in our world. The chemical symbol for carbon dioxide is CO_2, because it contains both carbon (C) and oxygen (O). Plants use CO_2 to make food during *photosynthesis*—a process that gives off oxygen, which animals breathe in to live and have energy. Carbon dioxide is released in small amounts by volcanoes when they erupt, and it is used to make bubbly beverages. Normally you can't see carbon dioxide, but you can see its effects in the following experiments.

TRY THIS
RAISIN BEBOP

Cola, ginger ale, seltzer water—these are all fun drinks because they're full of bubbles that tickle your throat when you drink them. And they can make you burp! But these drinks are fun in other ways, too!

QUESTION

What makes raisins dance in a glass of fizzy water?

WHAT YOU NEED

Can of clear soda—seltzer water or a lemon-lime soda works well
Tall see-through glass
Handful of raisins

WHAT TO DO

1. Fill the glass three-quarters of the way with soda.
2. Slip the raisins into the glass, one at a time.
3. What happens to the raisins?

WHAT'S HAPPENING

Soda water has more than just water in it. It has CO_2, a gas that creates the bubbles you see in the soda. When you dropped the raisins into the glass, they sank to the bottom and became coated in bubbles. This is because the surface of a raisin has little pockets. Those pockets trap bubbles of air that grab some of the carbon dioxide in the soda. The bubbles cause the raisins to rise to the top of the glass. Once the raisins reach the top of the glass, the bubbles pop, the carbon dioxide is released, and the raisins sink back to the bottom. The bubbles act like a life jacket, making the raisins more buoyant, which allows them to float and sink. If your raisins aren't sinking, give them a little tap to knock off the bubbles.

YOUR NOTES

Draw a picture of your be-bopping raisins.

What other foods could you use in this experiment? How about uncooked pasta or lemon seeds? What happens?

Way to Glow!

Mix together oxalate ester and fluorescent dye, add some hydrogen peroxide and shake. Something really amazing happens! What? You don't know what these chemicals are? Maybe not, but you have probably done this experiment more than once! Break the Letter Shift code to learn when that was.

D+1	W-1	G-2	N+4	X+1		V-2	H+1	H+5	5	
Z-1	N+1	N+7		A+2	T-2	C-2	3	C+8		
1	A+13	A+3		Q+2	D+4	D-3	H+3	A+4		H-7
M-6	M-1	15	Z-3		P+5	P+4	9	I-6	1+2	!

TRY THIS
DISSOLVING CHALK

You can draw all kinds of cool pictures with sidewalk chalk using different colors and sizes. Eventually the chalk sticks wear down as you use them. But did you know you can dissolve, or erode, chalk using a liquid?

QUESTION

How does a liquid dissolve a piece of chalk?

WHAT YOU NEED

Bowl
Vinegar (white or cider)
Blackboard chalk
Stopwatch

WHAT TO DO

1. Pour vinegar into the bowl so it's half full.
2. Drop the chalk into the bowl.
3. Start your stopwatch and observe what happens.
4. You may need to add more vinegar depending on the size of the chalk.
5. How long does it take for the chalk to start dissolving? Record the time in the Your Notes section.

WHAT'S HAPPENING

Chalk is made up of limestone, or calcium carbonate. The vinegar is made up of an acid called acetic acid. The acid eats away at the calcium carbonate, releasing bubbles of carbon dioxide. That is why you see bubbles forming around the chalk.

Limestone Caves

There are many caves that have been formed by carbonic acid dripping onto limestone over thousands of years. The acid slowly eats away at the stone, carving out the space for a cave. Limestone is made up of tiny pieces of sea shells and a mineral called calcite.

limestone: rock formed mostly by remains of sea shells and consisting of calcium carbonate.

FUN FACT

Giant Cave

Sarawak Chamber, in Malaysia, is the largest cave in the world. It is 2,300 feet long, 980 feet wide, and more than 230 feet high. When cavers discovered it, they couldn't see the end of their flashlight beam because the cave was so enormous!

In nature, carbon dioxide gas is always present in the air. And this gas can get into our rain, turning it slightly acidic. Usually this is not a problem, and this naturally acidic rain has helped shape many of the mountains and canyons in our landscape. However, now there's too much carbon dioxide in the atmosphere from our cars and our factories. And the rain has become too acidic, damaging forests and eroding our mountains.

YOUR NOTES

How long did it take for the chalk to start dissolving?

_____

Which Is Which?

Take three glasses of water. Add a few drops of vanilla to one glass, a drop of perfume to the next glass, and several drops of onion juice to the last. Look away and have a helper switch the glasses around. Can you think of an easy chemical reaction that will help you to tell which glass is which?

= S
= E
= L
= N
= O
= F
= M

SCIENCE LAB: BURPING BALLOON

Some caves are deep underground, and they don't have much oxygen. However, they do have a lot of carbon dioxide. But you don't know how much because CO_2 has no smell. There is a simple test you can do, and it's similar to the following experiment.

QUESTION

What gas can put out a flame?

WHAT YOU NEED

Adult	Teaspoon
Measuring cup	Baking soda
Vinegar	Clay
Small bottle	Wide jar
Funnel	Small candle
Balloon	Matches

WHAT TO DO

1. Pour about 1¾ ounces of vinegar into the small bottle.
2. Slide the bottom of the funnel into the mouth of the balloon.
3. Pour one teaspoon of baking soda into the balloon. To make sure all the baking soda made it into the balloon, gently shake the funnel. Remove funnel.
4. Hold the neck of the balloon closed and let the balloon fall to one side to keep the baking soda from falling out. Stretch the mouth of the balloon over the opening of the bottle.
5. Now hold the balloon upright so the baking soda falls into the vinegar. What happens to the baking soda? What happens to the balloon?
6. Watch the chemical reaction until you don't see any more bubbles.
7. What gas do you think is inside the balloon? Make a guess.
8. Now flatten a piece of clay and put it at the bottom of the jar.
9. Place the candle firmly into the clay so it stands up by itself.
10. Ask an adult to light the candle. Let it burn for a while so that the candle is short.
11. With the adult's help, pinch the neck of the balloon to hold in the gas, remove it from the bottle, and place it at the mouth of the jar with the candle. Slowly let go of the neck.
12. What happens to the flame?

WHAT'S HAPPENING

Mixing baking soda and vinegar causes a chemical reaction that creates carbon dioxide gas. Unlike oxygen, which makes a flame burn faster, and hydrogen, which also burns, carbon dioxide is used to put out fires. So when you released the balloon full of carbon dioxide, the candle flame went out.

It's important to always practice fire safety. Not all fires can be put out with just water. Make sure your kitchen has a fire extinguisher. It uses carbon dioxide to put out a fire.

In a deep underground cave, explorers called cavers will carry a butane lighter with them. If they are starting to have trouble breathing, they flick open the lighter and look at the flame. If the flame immediately goes out or doesn't appear at all, then they head straight back to the entrance. There is not enough oxygen in the cave for them to safely explore.

YOUR NOTES

Draw a picture of your experiment and label each part. You are making a diagram. You can use this drawing to recreate the experiment.

What other acidic liquids could you use? Try lemon juice, orange juice, or grapefruit juice.

Chemical Changes

Chemical changes happen in the world around us every day. When you boil a raw egg, you cook it and change its form. When food goes bad or a candle burns or a metal rusts, a chemical change has occurred. In a chemical change, you have a new product that you didn't have before. Perhaps now you have a new gas, a new odor, or sound, or heat. In the following experiments you'll see some pretty amazing chemical changes.

TRY THIS
OOBLECK

What's white and goopy and hard and drippy at the same time? Stumped? Do this experiment and you'll find out!

QUESTION

Can you create a substance that is both a liquid and a solid?

WHAT YOU NEED

Large bowl	Cornstarch
1-cup measure	Spoon
½-cup measure	Paper towels
Water	Food coloring

WORDS to KNOW

chemical change: a chemical process by which a new substance is created.

WHAT TO DO

1. Pour 1 cup water into the bowl.
2. Now add 1½ to 2 cups cornstarch to the water. Add it slowly and stir slowly. You want to mix in the cornstarch a little at a time.

3. If it becomes difficult to stir, just use your hands to mix up the water and cornstarch.
4. What do you notice is happening to the mixture?
5. When the water and cornstarch are thoroughly combined, and the mixture is not runny or powdery, you have made oobleck! Let it set for a few seconds.
6. Tap the top of the oobleck. What does it feel like?
7. Grab a handful of oobleck. What do you feel? Now slowly open your hand. What is the substance doing?
8. Use the paper towels to clean up any mess. If you like, add food coloring to make the oobleck even more fun.

WHAT'S HAPPENING

Matter, what things are made of, has four states: solid, liquid, gas, and plasma. In this experiment, you combined cornstarch, a solid, with water, a liquid. The cornstarch and water created a chemical change, resulting in a unique mixture that acts like a solid when it has pressure on it and acts like a liquid when it has no pressure. When you tapped the oobleck, it felt hard because you were putting pressure on it. When you grabbed it and then let go, the oobleck oozed out of your hand because you had released the pressure. You have made a substance that exists in two states of matter.

YOUR NOTES

Try putting the oobleck into a plastic container and hitting it against a table. What happens?

Try making a ball out of the oobleck. When you let go of the ball, what happens?

Try picking it up with a spoon or a slotted spatula. What happens?

Seuss Science

Oobleck is named for some very odd stuff that falls out of the sky in a book called Bartholomew and the Oobleck by Dr. Seuss.

TRY THIS
SPY SCHOOL

Ready for a top-secret assignment? In this experiment you're going to learn how a popular form of secret message is created so you can make your own. What will you write using your homemade invisible ink?

QUESTION

What makes invisible ink visible?

WHAT YOU NEED

Lemon juice
Cup
Paintbrush
Paper
Friend
Hot lamp

WHAT TO DO

1. Squeeze some lemon juice into a cup. Don't worry if there are seeds in the juice.
2. Dip your paintbrush into the lemon juice. Paint a message on the paper.
3. Let the lemon juice dry.
4. Now give the paper to a friend.
5. Have your friend hold the paper up to a lamp. What happens?

Why did the spy send a secret message using lemon juice?

Because he thought it would be a-peel-ing!

43

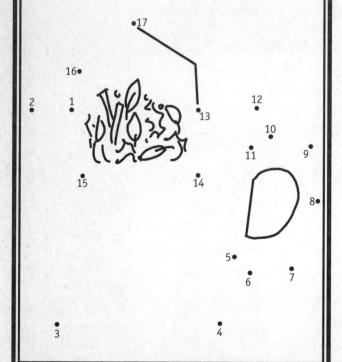

Tasty

A chemist has a pile of tasty and nice smelling leaves. She wants to use the flavor and aroma but keep the dry and woody parts of the leaves separate. Connect the dots to find out one way she can do this!

WHAT'S HAPPENING

When you applied the lemon juice to the paper, you could probably see your writing at first, but then the juice dried and your writing disappeared. Presto! Your message was hidden.

To make your message appear, you held the paper close to the lamp. The heat in the lamp caused a chemical change—the water molecules in the lemon juice evaporated from the heat, leaving behind sugar molecules. The sugar molecules reacted to the oxygen in the air and turned brown, revealing the secret note.

Secret messages can be made and revealed using all kinds of methods. Ultraviolet light, for instance, is used by the United States Postal Service to print routing information on packages. The information is not visible without an ultraviolet light.

Sometimes, even though a message is "invisible," it is still possible to tell that a blank piece of paper isn't really blank. If you look carefully, you might just see the juice sitting on top of the paper.

YOUR NOTES

Try this experiment with other citric acids, such as orange juice and grapefruit juice. Do they work as well as the lemon juice did?

SCIENCE LAB:
STOVETOP PLASTIC

Quite a few of the things we use every day are made of plastic. And they are usually made in a factory using chemicals. But hiding in your fridge and cabinets are two ingredients that, when put together, make a simple kind of plastic that can be molded and decorated.

QUESTION

How do you make plastic?

WHAT YOU NEED

Pint of milk
Adult
Saucepan
Mixing spoon
1-teaspoon measure
White vinegar
Sieve
Large pan
Rubber gloves
Water

WHAT TO DO

1. Pour milk into the saucepan.
2. Ask an adult to turn on the stove and put the saucepan on the stove.
3. Simmer the milk, but don't let it burn.
4. Carefully measure out 4 teaspoons vinegar and pour them into the milk. Don't touch the hot pan.
5. What do you see in the pan? Stir the mixture.
6. Ask an adult to turn off the heat and set the pan aside to let the mixture cool.
7. Put the sieve into a larger pan.
8. Ask an adult to pour the mixture into the sieve, letting the liquid run down the drain. What do you have left in the sieve?
9. Put on the gloves and wash the blobs under cool running water. When they're cool, press them with your hands. What do they feel like? What do they smell like?
10. Now you have your own plastic. Make it into some fun shapes and let it dry for a day. Then you can decorate it!

WHAT'S HAPPENING

Milk contains a protein called casein. This protein is not something you can taste in regular milk. But when you add an acid, such as vinegar, and heat, the protein turns into lumps. These lumps are similar to the plastic used in almost everything we own. This chemical change is a big one—don't eat the lumps, they're not made of milk anymore and it's not safe!

YOUR NOTES

Describe the smell and feel of the plastic you just made.

_____
_____
_____

What did you make with your plastic? Draw a picture of it here.

protein: an essential part of the food we eat that helps our bodies grow healthy and strong.

FUN FACT

Yummy Cheese

An Indian cheese called paneer is made by adding lemon juice to milk. But the cheese curds are soft and edible, unlike the plastic you made.

Light

Light is all around us. We see light from a lamp, from a flashlight, from a candle, and most of all from the sun. If you hold a ribbon in one hand and shake it up and down quickly, you can see short waves along the ribbon. Those waves are how we get light and heat from the sun.

TRY THIS
FLASHLIGHT FUN

Flashlights can be used for making scary faces at a dark campsite, finding your way through your house at night, and...doing cool experiments!

QUESTION

How far does light shine?

WHAT YOU NEED

Medium-sized flashlight
Measuring tape
Friend
2 small mirrors

WHAT TO DO

1. Grab a friend and a flashlight.
2. Turn off the light in your room and stand at one end.
3. Turn on the flashlight. Shine the beam on a white or light-colored wall.
4. Have your friend measure the distance of the beam from the flashlight to the point where it shines on the opposite

WORDS to KNOW

reflection: when light waves bounce back from a surface.

refraction: when light bends because it passes through a substance such as glass or water.

FUN FACT

Lickety-Split Light

Did you know that light travels faster than sound? Light travels at about 186,000 miles per second, or 300,000 kilometers per second. Sound only travels at about 0.2 miles per second, or 340 meters per second. That's why, for example, you usually see fireworks before you hear them.

wall. Write the number in the following Your Notes section.

5. Go to a hallway. Have your friend count his steps to the other end of the hallway.

6. Before you turn on the flashlight, do you think the beam will reach him? Now turn on the flashlight and aim the beam at his shirt. Were you right? Write down the number of steps in the following Your Notes section.

7. At night, shine your flashlight up into the sky. Does it look like your beam reaches the stars?

8. Now set up two mirrors across from each other.

9. Shine the flashlight into one mirror so that the beam bounces off and shines into the other mirror. What do you notice about the brightness of the beam?

FUN FACT

Bright History

In colonial times, people used candles to light their houses. But candles didn't put out much light by themselves. So people put mirrors behind the candles to make the light shine brighter.

WHAT'S HAPPENING

The light we see travels in rays that move very fast in a straight line. The speed of light is 186,000 miles per second. That means light travels from the Sun, which is 93,000,000 miles away, to the Earth in eight minutes!

So when you shine the flashlight at a wall, you are seeing light rays hit the wall and bounce off, or reflect. Light travels until it hits something and reflects back, even up into the night sky. And when you use mirrors, you increase the brightness of the light rays because they are bouncing back and forth between the mirrors. No part of the beam is reflecting away and making the light dimmer.

Invisible Filler

Even though you can't see it, air is more than just nothingness! Air is a gas made up of molecules that fills any container it is inside. Let's test this idea—you will need a piece of newspaper or tissue paper, an empty drinking glass or glass jar, and a deep pot (like a soup kettle) full of water. To learn the directions for this experiment, use the numbered words to fill in the blanks.

_____ the paper.
10

_____ it _____ deep
1   9

____ the glass. Hold
3

the ____ so the _____
5   2

is facing ____, and
8

push it slowly ____ the
3

____. Hold it there for
7

a _____. Carefully pull
4

the ____ out of the
5

_____ and _____ the
7   6

paper.

1. **STUFF**
2. **MOUTH**
3. **INTO**
4. **MINUTE**
5. **GLASS**
6. **REMOVE**
7. **WATER**
8. **DOWN**
9. **TIGHTLY**
10. **CRUMPLE**

YOUR NOTES

My room

_____

My hallway

_____

TRY THIS
FLIP-FLOP ABC

Mirrors are tricky things. They can make us see our world very differently. They can make things appear that aren't there, and they can distort our understanding of how close or far away something is.

QUESTION

Why do things appear differently in a mirror?

WHAT YOU NEED

Medium-sized flat mirror
Sheet of paper
Pencil

WHAT TO DO

1. Write the alphabet in capital letters on the paper.
2. Hold the mirror above the alphabet. You should be able to see the letters in the mirror.

Picture of me shining my flashlight up at the stars.

WORDS to KNOW

palindrome: a word that reads the same forward and backward.

3. Do the letters look different? Do some look the same?
4. Now write the following words on the paper:
   POP   EYE   TOOT   LEVEL
5. Place the mirror at the end of each word so the word appears in the mirror. Do you notice anything about each word?

WHAT'S HAPPENING

A mirror is made out of a metal or glass that has been coated with a thin layer of silver or aluminum. The surface of a mirror acts as a reflector. Mirrors reflect letters that are horizontally symmetrical. This means the letters can be cut across the

Mega Mirror

Can you imagine a mirror that is so big there isn't a place on Earth where it would fit? Believe it or not, there is such a mirror—and you have seen it! Break the Vowel Scramble code to learn what it is and how it works.

Thu meen octs laku o gagontac marrer. Ot mokus ne laght ef ats ewn — meenlaght as jist sinlaght beincang eff thu sirfocu ef thu meen!

middle and have the same top and bottom half. An H is an example of a horizontally symmetrical letter. The letters that look backward in the mirror are ones that are not horizontally symmetrical, such as V or R. Palindromes, such as POP and EYE are words that read the same forward and backward, a different kind of symmetry. These words read just fine in a mirror.

Mirrors were originally just pools of water that, when still, produced a reflected but slightly distorted image. The most common mirrors are flat mirrors. But some mirrors are curved inward, called concave mirrors. And other mirrors curve outward, giving them a convex shape, They allow you to see a wider area than flat mirrors do. Large trucks use convex mirrors to see around their wide back ends. Parking garages place convex mirrors at their exits so that drivers can see any pedestrians walking nearby.

YOUR NOTES

What other palindromes can you think of?

_____
_____
_____
_____

What secret messages can you write in your new backward code?

_____
_____
_____

Cool Quotes

Equipped with his five senses, man explores the universe around him and calls the adventure Science.

—Edwin Powell Hubble

Why did the young scientist study in a hot air balloon?

He wanted a higher education!

SCIENCE LAB:
PAPER PERISCOPE

Have you ever played a game of hide-and-seek and wished you could see someone coming without being seen yourself? You can, with the help of an instrument called a periscope.

QUESTION

How can you peer around a corner or look over a wall?

WHAT YOU NEED

Empty milk carton
Tape
Ruler
Pencil
2 small square mirrors
Scissors or a box cutter

WHAT TO DO

1. Ask a grownup to cut one hole at the top of one side of the carton and a second hole at the bottom of the other side of the carton. The holes should be about the same size.
2. Use tape to seal the opening of the carton.
3. Turn the carton to a side without holes.
4. Draw a square at the same level as the bottom hole. Ask a grownup to help you draw a diagonal line across the square at a 45-degree angle.
5. Do the same thing at the level of the top hole. Then turn the carton to the remaining side without holes and draw two more squares and two more lines.
6. Ask a grownup to cut a slit along the diagonal lines.
7. Insert one mirror into the bottom slit. Insert the other mirror, reflective side down, into the top slit.
8. Now find a spot to try out your new periscope. What do you see?

WHAT'S HAPPENING

A periscope is an instrument that allows you to see what's going on around you even though you're hidden. It works with light rays and angles. When light reflects off the surface of the top mirror of the periscope, the light rays change direction and then reflect off of the bottom mirror. This allows you to see what is going on way above you or around a corner.

54

Your periscope may seem very simple, but this model was used in World War I. Soldiers would put the periscopes on their rifles so that they could duck down in the trenches and stay safe but still see what was going on around them. Submarines also use periscopes, though those models are much more powerful. A submarine sends up its periscope while the vessel is still underwater, thereby allowing it to remain hidden from view while the captain scopes out the surface of the water.

YOUR NOTES

Draw what you see with your periscope.

What a Drag!

Scientists have a name for the force that slows an object down as it moves through the air. It is called "drag." Use the picture equations to sound out directions for an experiment. Which object shows more drag?

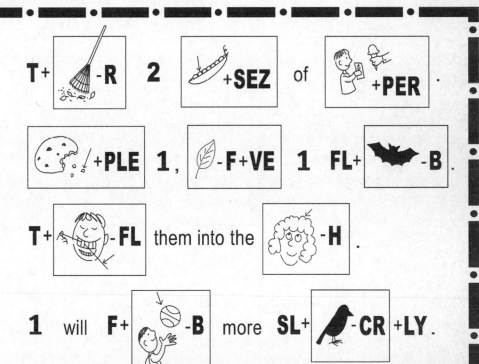

Surface Tension and Buoyancy

We live in a wet world. About 70 percent of the Earth is covered in oceans. We drink and bathe in tap water, and we use water to keep our landscapes green and healthy. Our bodies are mostly made up of water.

Water has unique properties. It holds itself together in a bubble and pushes up on boats as they float. It can be a solid ice cube; a liquid; or a gas, as water vapor.

TRY THIS
PLENTY OF PINS

Did you know that water has its own kind of skin? Bodies of water have a thin layer on the surface that is both extremely fragile and yet strong. Teeny tiny insects can flit across the top of a pond, but your boot splashes straight to the bottom of a mud puddle. What property does water have to make this "skin"?

QUESTION

How many pins can you add to a full glass of water before it overflows?

WHAT YOU NEED

Large handful of straight pins (be careful not to stick yourself)
Drinking glass
Water

WORDS to KNOW

gravity: the force that holds objects close to the Earth's surface. On the Moon there is no gravity, and objects just float around.

WHAT TO DO

1. Fill the glass to the brim with water.
2. Carefully slip a pin into the glass.
3. Add another. How many do you think you can add before the water spills over? Write your guess in the following Your Notes section.
4. As you add pins, bend down so you can see the level of the water in the glass. Do you see the level rising above the top of the glass?
5. Don't forget to count how many pins you are dropping.
6. Keep adding pins until the glass overflows. Write the total number of pins in the following Your Notes section.

WHAT'S HAPPENING

Did you think the glass would overflow right away? Were you surprised when it didn't? The surface of the water has tension, which means the molecules are attracted to each other and exert a force on each other. That attraction pushes the molecules toward the center of the water, giving it an elastic "surface." Surface tension explains why bubbles and raindrops hold together, and why something like a paper clip, which is denser than water, can rest flat on the surface of the water without sinking.

In this experiment, surface tension kept the water from flowing out of the glass even once you added a lot of pins.

YOUR NOTES

My guess:

_____

Actual number of pins I used:

Water Walker

There is an insect, called a water strider, that can walk on water. Its legs have tiny hairs that hold air bubbles. These allow the insect to float on top of the water.

surface tension: the force that holds water molecules together and allows water to have a kind of skin.

Slo-Mo Rainbow

Here is a simple way to get a better look at the surface tension of a liquid. To learn how to do this experiment, use the directions to cross words out of the grid. When you are done, read the remaining words from left to right, top to bottom.

Cross out words that...
...rhyme with WET
...start with SA
...have a double P

3 drops yellow

3 drops green

3 drops red

SAMPLE	POUR	ONE	BET	CUP
MILK	GET	INTO	A	NET
SET	SHALLOW	COPPER	BOWL	WAIT
UNTIL	MILK	IS	SALTY	STILL
SADDLE	CAREFULLY	SAT	ADD	LET
FOOD	COLOR	POPPED	ZIPPY	IN
SASH	HAPPEN	PATTERN	SHOWN	SAUCE
ADD	ONE	JET	TIPPED	DROP
PET	OF	LIQUID	MET	SOAP
IN	DRIPPY	THE	MIDDLE	VET

WHAT SINKS? WHAT FLOATS?

The next time you're in a swimming pool, try just being still in the water. Do you sink to the bottom or float like a cork? What about the toys you bring to the pool?

QUESTION

Which objects sink? Which ones float? Why?

WHAT YOU NEED

Kitchen sink with a drain stopper
Whole lemon
Lemon slice
Whole lime
Lime slice
Sponge
Half strand of dried spaghetti
Whole orange
Orange peel
Peeled orange
Anything else you want to try

WHAT TO DO

1. Put the stopper in the drain and fill the sink almost full of water.
2. Place the lemon into the sink. Did it sink or float? Mark your answer in the Your Notes section.
3. Continue with each item, one at a time.

Bloop

Search the letter grid for the names of four items found in a kitchen. Use the words to fill in the blanks. Follow the directions to observe density in action!

```
B E N D J U B
S S A L G D W
L N X U K S A
Q U N S N U T
X K L A X F E
N O I L J N R
D S U T N Q U
```

Take the G_ _ _ _.
Fill it two-thirds with W_ _ _ _. Pour in a quarter inch of O_ _. Pour in an eighth of a cup of S_ _ _.

What happens? Can you guess why?

59

4. Did any objects surprise you? Find some other items you'd like to try.
5. When you're done, pull out all the objects and use the water for something else, like washing dishes.

WHAT'S HAPPENING

Pick up the orange and the lime. The orange feels heavier, right? When you placed the whole orange in the water, you probably expected it to sink, because its weight felt greater when you held it. But instead, it floated and the lime, which initially felt lighter, sank to the bottom. What's going on?

When an object is in water, the water exerts an upward force on the object. This force is called buoyancy. The amount of this force is equal to the weight of the water that is displaced, or pushed aside, by the object. If the buoyancy exerted on the object is greater than the weight of the object, it rises until it breaks the surface of the water. At this point, the buoyant force on the object is equal to its weight and it floats. If the buoyancy of an object is less than its weight, it sinks.

volume: the measurement of the space taken up by an object.

In this experiment, the weight of the orange displaced a volume of water that was less than the volume of the orange. Volume is a measurement of the space taken up by an object. The orange took up more space than the water it displaced, so the orange rose in the water until it reached the surface and floated. In the case of the lime, its buoyancy was less than its weight, so it sank.

As for the peeled orange, the peel increases the buoyant force on the orange through tiny air pockets. These pockets helped the orange stay afloat.

YOUR NOTES

Whole lemon _____

_____

Lemon slice _____

_____

Whole lime _____

_____

Lime slice _____

_____

Sponge _____

_____

Spaghetti _____

_____

Whole orange _____

_____

Peeled orange _____

_____

Other items _____

_____

_____

FUN FACT

Into the Deep

A huge submarine can submerge, also known as diving, underwater by filling special tanks with water, making it heavier. When it wants to rise, it replaces the water with air.

WORDS to KNOW

elastic: able to be stretched and then returned to the original shape.

SCIENCE LAB:
BUBBLE BUILDER

Whether you're blowing bubbles with soap, chewing gum, or a straw in a milk glass, these translucent, round balls are fun to play with. They grow and shrink depending on how much air you blow into them. They pop with a satisfying sound and spray, and they sometimes have rainbows in them. But did you know you can build with them?

QUESTION

Are bubbles always round?

WHAT YOU NEED

Bubble solution (see following steps)
Flat tray
Straw

BUBBLE SOLUTION

You will need:
1 gallon water
⅔ cup dishwashing liquid
1 tablespoon glycerine (you can find this at drug stores)

1. Pour the water and dishwashing liquid into a container. Mix well.
2. Add the glycerine. If you don't have it, that's okay. But it will make your bubbles stronger.

WHAT TO DO

1. Pour some bubble solution onto the tray. Make sure the bottom of the tray is completely covered.
2. Put your straw into the bubble solution. Blow gently through the straw. What do you see?
3. Gently place your bubble onto the tray without popping it. What shape is your bubble?
4. Dip your straw back into the solution and blow another bubble. Watch what happens when you place it on top of the first bubble. Are they still round?
5. If your bubble pops, don't worry. Just make another one.
6. Keep blowing bubbles. What shapes do you see where the bubbles come together?

WHAT'S HAPPENING

Bubble solution is essentially soap. And soap has surface tension, the force you learned about in the pin experiment. The molecules are trying to hold themselves together as tightly as possible. That's why you see a film on the surface of the soap mixture. But that film is elastic.

When you blow a bubble, you stretch the water molecules into a sphere around the air in the bubble, making the bubble round. Bubbles are usually round. But where the bubbles touch each other, their shapes change and become flat, as the molecules keep squeezing together.

YOUR NOTES

Draw a picture of your bubble construction. How high can you build it?

Magnets and Electricity

Magnets can be big or small. Tiny magnets can hold your artwork on the fridge. A compass magnet is able to point to the Earth's magnetic north pole. Magnets have a magnetic field around them. This magnetic field can create electricity, using a device like a generator.

Turn on a flashlight, a toaster, or a TV. All these things use electricity. Electricity is made when positive and negative charges come into contact with each other. Nowadays, there are even some cars that can run only on electricity.

TRY THIS
MAGNET MANIA

Scientists often use a problem-solving method called "trial and error" to discover the answer to a question. They form a *hypothesis*, otherwise known as a guess, which provides them with a possibility for an answer. And then they think of ways to test that hypothesis to see if they were correct. You are going to do an experiment built around the method of trial and error. Do you like this approach to answering a question?

QUESTION

What makes some magnets stick together and other magnets pull apart? And why do magnets stick to some things and not to others?

WHAT YOU NEED

2 hard magnets (flexible magnets don't work as well)

FUN FACT

Twice the Attraction

Did you know that if you break a magnet in half, you don't have two north poles or two south poles, but two brand new magnets, each with one north pole and one south pole!

What is the brightest city in the world?

Electri-city!

WHAT TO DO

1. Point the two magnets at each other. What do you notice? Do they stick together right away or do they seem to push away from each other?
2. If they stick together, then turn one around. Now point it at the other magnet. What happens?
3. Take the magnets around the house and see what surfaces and objects they stick to. You might try the following list first, and then think of your own ideas. Make a check mark next to each item in the list that is magnetic.

WHAT'S HAPPENING

A magnet has two sides to it, called poles. One side is the north pole, the other side is the south pole. The rule to remember is opposites attract. The north pole of one magnet will attract, or stick to, the south pole of another magnet. But the north pole of a magnet will repel, or push away, the north pole of another magnet. When a magnet sticks to a surface, we call that surface "magnetic." In this experiment, you tested how magnetic various surfaces and objects are in your house.

YOUR NOTES

Bedroom door_____

Bathroom mirror _____

Metal fork _____

Plastic spoon_____

Cast iron pan _____

Penny _____

Nickel _____

Keys_____

Key rings _____

FUN FACT

Pole Position

The Earth has two magnetic poles: North and South. And their magnetic pull is quite strong. Scientists believe birds rely on this magnetic field to find their way during migration.

WORDS to KNOW

magnet: a mass of iron or steel or some mixture of both that can attract iron and that produces a magnetic field.

Plus and Minus

Each magnet has a north pole and a south pole, and each pole is attracted to its opposite. See if you can make a path through this maze alternating between signs that are opposites. Start on the plus (+) sign, then travel to a minus (-) sign. Rules: You can travel side to side or up and down, but not diagonally. If you come to an X, you are going the wrong way!

Kitchen faucet _____

Fridge _____

Cabinet _____

Oven door (make sure it isn't hot!)_____

(Careful: don't ever stick magnets to electronic equipment, including music players, computers, and TVs. Magnets can damage these appliances.)

TRY THIS
ZAP!

Have you ever pulled on a sweater in winter and then touched a doorknob? Did you feel a jolt in your fingertips? Or have you ever touched someone's hand and felt a zap? That's static electricity.

QUESTION

What causes static electricity?

WHAT YOU NEED

Socks
Carpet
Metal doorknob
Balloon

WHAT TO DO

1. Put on the socks.
2. Shuffle your feet across the carpet for a few seconds.

Big Bolts

One bolt of lightning can measure 3 million volts in just one second. A spark of static electricity can equal 3,000 volts.

WORDS to KNOW

static electricity: electricity caused by rubbing two objects together.

FUN FACT

Bird on a Wire

Have you ever looked up and seen a bird sitting on a telephone wire? Ever wonder how the bird can safely sit on a wire that conducts electricity? As long as no part of the bird is touching the ground, the current passes right through the bird without hurting it. You, on the other hand, should never go near a power line.

3. Touch a metal doorknob. What happens? Make sure the doorknob is the first thing you touch after you shuffle your feet.
4. Blow up the balloon and tie it.
5. Rub the balloon on your hair and then pull it away slowly. What happens to your hair?
6. Now stick the balloon to a nearby wall and let go. Does it stick to the wall?

WHAT'S HAPPENING

When you shuffle your feet on a carpet and rub the balloon on your hair, you're putting something on it called negative charges. Charges can be positive or negative. Like a magnet, two positive charges repel each other, but a positive charge and a negative charge attract each other. You build up these charges as long as you don't touch anything. Once you do, you release the charges onto another surface. And that's what causes the zap. When you then placed the balloon against the wall, the negative charges in the balloon were attracted to the positive charges on the wall. So they stuck together!

Static electricity usually isn't dangerous. It's a tiny charge. But there are times when it's a problem. At gas stations, there sometimes are signs telling drivers to touch their cars before filling their gas tanks. A driver can build up static electricity from the seat in his car and then release those charges on the gasoline hose. This can cause a fire. It is important to always be safe when using electricity.

YOUR NOTES

Draw a picture of yourself with static electricity in your hair.

SCIENCE LAB: LOCAL POWER

Many of your toys and appliances use batteries. Batteries come in all types with many different names: AA, AAA, C, D, 9-volt. But inside all those batteries are components that generate a charge. You can gather those components and put them together to make your own, small power. What name would you give your very own battery?

QUESTION

How do you make a homemade battery?

WHAT YOU NEED

Potato Battery
Potato
Penny
Piece of aluminum foil

Lemon Battery
Lemon
Galvanized steel nail
Copper nail

Volta's Pile
6 pennies
6 paper towel circles
Plate
6 circles of aluminum foil
Salt water (1 teaspoon salt dissolved in 6 ounces of water)

Other Items
Knife
Voltmeter (can be purchased at local electronics store)

WHAT TO DO

Potato Battery
1. Ask a grownup to cut two slits in the potato.
2. Insert the penny into the first slit. It's best to use a penny that was made after 1982. It will have a higher concentration of copper.
3. Insert the piece of foil into the second slit. Make sure the penny and foil don't touch while they're in the potato. They could short out, or break, the battery.
4. Pick up the probes that are attached to the voltmeter. Touch one probe to the copper penny and the other probe to the foil.

5. Look at the voltmeter screen. What number do you see? Write it on the line in the following Your Notes section. The numbers on the voltmeter may jump around a bit, so hold the probes still and wait until they slow down.
6. Try pushing the penny and foil deep into the potato to make sure they are making contact with the juice of the potato.

Lemon Battery

1. Ask a grownup to cut two slits in the lemon.
2. Insert the copper nail into the first slit.
3. Insert the steel nail into the second slit.
4. Touch one probe to the copper nail and the other to the steel nail.
5. What voltage do you see? Record the number in the following Your Notes section. Is it very different from the potato battery?
6. Try rolling the lemon on the counter. This helps release the juice.

Volta's Pile

1. Soak the six paper towel circles in the salt solution. Carefully take them out and lay them on a plate.
2. Take one penny, put a towel circle on top of the penny, and then place a foil circle on top of the towel circle.

3. Keep doing this until you've used all the pieces.
4. Squeeze the battery together and set it on its side. Make sure all the pieces hold together.
5. Touch one probe to the copper side of the pile. Touch the other probe to the foil side of the pile. What does the voltmeter say? Record the number in the following Your Notes section.

WHAT'S HAPPENING

In 1800, a man named Alessandro Volta discovered that if he put copper and zinc together with a wet paper in between, he could generate a certain amount of voltage. That construction is known as Volta's pile, and it generated about 1 volt, named after him.

A battery is made up of cells similar to Volta's pile. And each cell contains one half-cell with electrolyte and a positive electrode and a second half-cell with electrolyte and a negative electrode. The electrolyte helps move the charge from the negative and positive electrodes through the battery.

In your batteries, the copper and zinc are the electrodes, and the lemon, the potato, and the salt water solution are all acting as electrolytes. You use a voltmeter to measure the voltage and current produced by each battery.

YOUR NOTES

Potato Battery Voltage: _____
_____
_____

Lemon Battery Voltage: _____
_____
_____

Volta's Pile Voltage: _____
_____
_____

Which battery generates the most voltage? _____
_____
_____

FUN FACT

Eel-ectric!

The electric eel causes quite a shock. It can produce 600 volts of electricity—enough to kill fish for a meal and scare off predators!

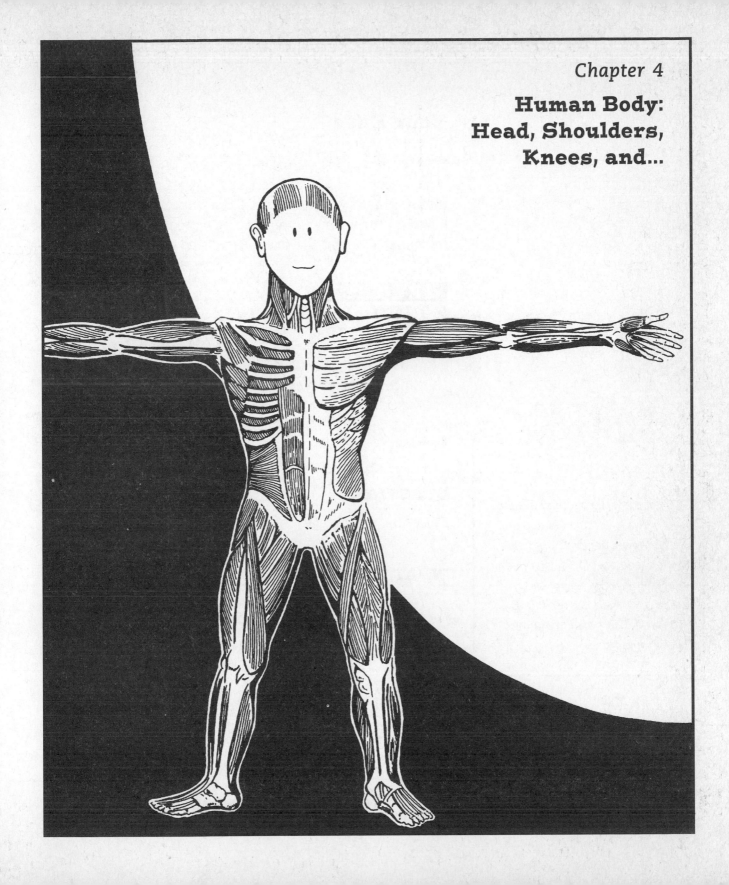

Chapter 4

Human Body: Head, Shoulders, Knees, and...

Your Ears

Touch your ears. What do they feel like? Curvy and spiraled? Your ears are designed to capture vibrations in the air caused by sound waves. These vibrations are amplified inside the inner ear and then passed on to the brain, which recognizes or learns the sound. That is how you hear.

TRY THIS
SOUND SLEUTH

Close your eyes. Do you hear any sounds nearby? Have you ever been in complete silence? It's pretty difficult to experience that since there's always some kind of noise going on around us—a dog barking, a car honking, a bird chirping, a breeze blowing, your breathing. Our ears tell us amazing things about what's going on in our world.

QUESTION

Can you tell where a sound is coming from?

WHAT YOU NEED

A friend

WHAT TO DO

1. Find a big room or go outside.
2. Close your eyes.
3. Have your friend stand a little ways away from you and make a sound. You can choose from the list in the Your Notes section or think of your own sounds.

FUN FACT

Fake Effects

Did you know that sometimes the sounds you hear on the radio and in the movies are fake? On radio shows, wooden blocks can imitate horses' hooves. In the movies, sound effects people use things like large sheets of aluminum to mimic thunder.

4. Point to where you think the sound is coming from.
5. Open your eyes. Were you right?
6. Now close your eyes again and ask your friend to stand to one side or the other and make another sound. Point again.
7. Try covering only one ear. When your friend makes a sound, is it easier or harder to hear it? Try the other ear.
8. Switch with your friend. Try standing really far away or really close. But be careful not to make a loud sound if you're close to your friend. You can damage her ear!
9. Try making the sound from up above or down below.

FUN FACT

Did You Hear?

Some animals have unique ways of hearing the world around them. Crickets use thin layers of skin on their legs to hear. Bats and dolphins send out sounds that bounce off of objects around them and make echoes. The echoes indicate how far away the objects are. Dolphins have much better hearing than humans—14 times better in fact!

WORDS to KNOW

echolocation: using echoes to determine the location of something. Bats and dolphins rely on echolocation to find their way.

WHAT'S HAPPENING

You were able to tell which direction the sounds were coming from because you have one ear on each side of your head. If your friend was standing on your left side, your left ear heard a louder sound than your right ear did. Your brain can tell the difference. If you heard a sound that was far away, your brain processed the time it took for the sound to reach you and figured out that the sound did not happen nearby.

Your ears also help you keep your balance. They contain a liquid that moves and presses against nerve endings in your ears as you move. This movement tells your brain that your body is in motion. If you spin very fast, the liquid pushes the hairs on the nerve endings in all different directions, disorienting your brain. So you feel dizzy. Your brain is confused about which way is up.

Many animals rely on their hearing to tell them if predators or prey are nearby. Certain owls have special feathers, called *ruff*, that channel sound up to their large ear holes, enabling them to hear very well. This helps them hunt at night when visibility is not as good. Owls' brains also do what our brains do and calculate the time it takes for sound to reach each ear. They can judge the distance of their prey based on that calculation.

YOUR NOTES

Hum
Clap
Whistle
Stomp
Yell
Whisper

Open and Shut

The directions for this exper-eye-ment are in a grid that has been cut into pieces. Match the pattern of black squares, and figure out where each piece goes. Then write the letters into the empty grid. To complete the experiment you will need a bathroom with a mirror and light over the sink.

pupil

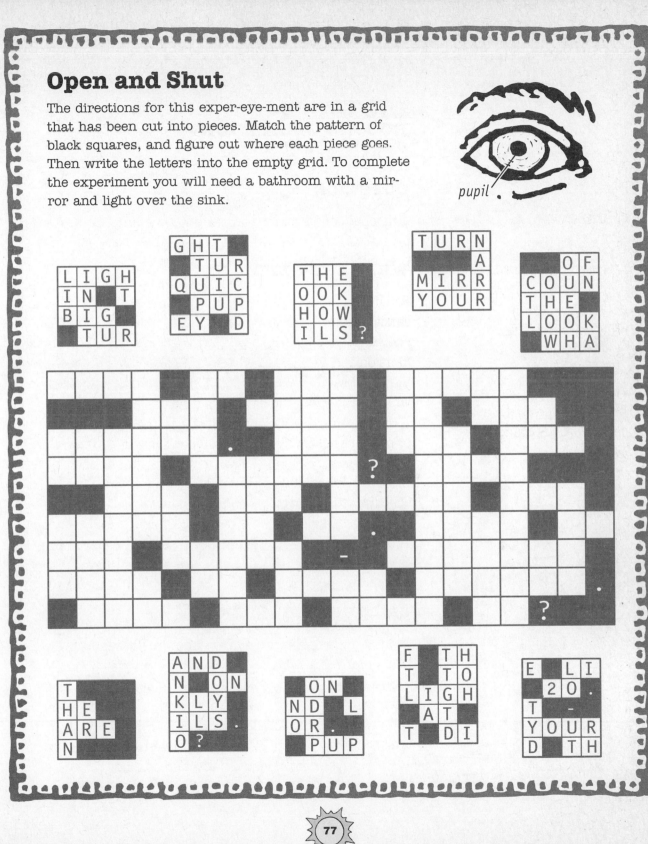

TRY THIS
BOOMING BALLOON

QUESTION

Can a balloon help you hear better?

WHAT YOU NEED

A balloon
A friend

WHAT TO DO

1. Blow up the balloon and tie it.
2. Hold the balloon against one ear. Tap gently on the balloon. Make sure you don't pop it. That would hurt your ear.
3. What do you hear?
4. Now have a friend talk against one side of the balloon.
5. Put your ear against the other side. Can you hear your friend? Does his voice sound different?

WHAT'S HAPPENING

Sound begins with a vibration in the air and travels to your ear in waves. When you blew up the balloon, you pushed the molecules of air into a small space. Sound waves pass more easily through this compressed air, which is why you heard a loud sound through the balloon. If you were to tap lightly on a balloon that is not near your ear, it would not sound as loud.

Sounds have pitch, which indicates how high or low the sound is. A tiny bell makes a high-pitched sound, while a big bell makes a low-pitched sound. You have a higher-pitched voice than your father does, for instance, even if you're a boy.

But sometimes this pitch can seem to shift, especially when it's coming from a moving object, like a fire truck or a police siren. What's happening is that your ear is first detecting long sound waves, which have a low pitch. This is usually when the police car is far away. Then as the car and its siren get closer, the waves get shorter and shorter, raising the pitch. As the car then passes you by, the waves get longer and longer again, dropping the pitch as the car drives away.

YOUR NOTES

Where can you take your balloon amplifier to hear high-pitched sounds? How about low-pitched sounds? Can you feel the balloon vibrating, too?

TRY THIS
TELE-CUP

Now that you know how sound moves, let's put those waves to work!

QUESTION

Sound can travel through the air, but can it travel along a string?

WHAT YOU NEED

Two plastic cups	10 feet of string
Scissors	Friend

WORDS to KNOW

vibrate: to move back and forth, or to and fro, rhythmically and rapidly.

FUN FACT

Sounds in the Earth

Plates in the Earth's crust are constantly in motion. Sometimes they push up against each other and cause an earthquake. The force of an earthquake sends sound waves rippling through the ground. Scientists called seismologists *use a seismograph to measure those waves and determine the strength of the quake.*

WORDS to KNOW

amplifier: something that amplifies, or increases, current, voltage, or power.

What's as big as a person but weighs nothing?

Its shadow!

WHAT TO DO

1. Ask an adult to use the scissors to poke a hole in the bottom of each cup.
2. Pull one end of the string through the hole in one cup and tie a knot. Do the same with the other cup and the other end of the string.
3. Give one cup to a friend. Tell him to hold the cup up to his ear. Then take the other cup and stand far enough away so that the string is pulled tight.
4. Now talk into your cup. Can your friend hear what you're saying?
5. Tell your friend to talk into his cup. Hold your cup up to your ear. Can you hear your friend?

WHAT'S HAPPENING

When you pull the string tight and talk into the cup, the vibrations in your voice travel down the string to the other cup. Your friend's ears receive the vibrations and his brain processes them into the words you said. And just like that, you have your very own telephone!

A regular telephone has its own little brain, translating sound waves into electrical signals and then translating them back into sound waves, creating a two-way exchange of sound. Telephones have come in all kinds of designs, some with handsets that are wired to a body with a rotating dial, others with handsets that are separate from the bodies, and now cellular telephones that receive wireless signals.

YOUR NOTES

Try talking quietly into your telephone. How low can you whisper and still be heard by your friend?

Try using different materials to make your phone—metal cans and fishing wire, for instance. Do you notice a difference? Make sure the metal cans are safe and don't have any sharp edges.

Try using cups that are different sizes. Try loosening the string. What happens?

Cool Quotes

Why are things the way they are and not otherwise?

—Johannes Kepler

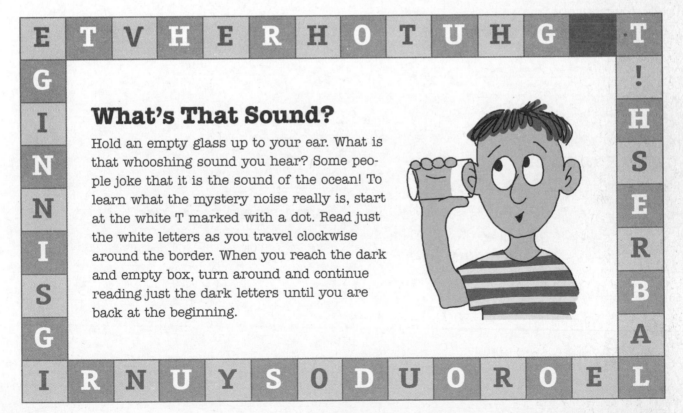

What's That Sound?

Hold an empty glass up to your ear. What is that whooshing sound you hear? Some people joke that it is the sound of the ocean! To learn what the mystery noise really is, start at the white T marked with a dot. Read just the white letters as you travel clockwise around the border. When you reach the dark and empty box, turn around and continue reading just the dark letters until you are back at the beginning.

SCIENCE LAB:
THE VANISHING FLAME

So now we know that sound moves in waves, the waves can be long and short, sound can have a high pitch and a low pitch, and our ears send signals to our brain about the nature of a sound and its location. But what if we could actually see sound moving?

QUESTION

Can you see sound waves?

WHAT YOU NEED

Scissors
Cardboard tube
Cellophane tape
Enough plastic wrap to fit around the top and bottom of the tube
Small candle

WHAT TO DO

1. Tear off several small strips of tape and attach them to the edge of the table so you can get to them easily.
2. Stretch some plastic wrap around the top of the tube. The wrap should extend over the open area.
3. Place some tape to secure the wrap in place. Do the same for the bottom of the tube.

4. Use the scissors to poke a hole in one end of the tube.
5. Ask a grownup to light the candle and hold it.
6. Hold the tube about an inch away from the flame. The end with the hole should face the flame. Be careful not to burn yourself or the tube.
7. Lightly tap the plastic wrap on the end away from the flame. What happened to the flame?
8. Have a grownup relight the flame. Can you tap lightly enough so that the flame doesn't go out?

WHAT'S HAPPENING

Sound waves are not visible, normally. But when you tapped the plastic wrap, the air inside the tube vibrated. The vibrations were strong enough to travel through the hole and blow out the flame. So you can see the effects of sound waves.

82

Another way you can detect sound is by feeling it. Touch the small bump at your throat while you say "Hello" a few times. Can you feel vibrations through your skin? We have two sections of stretchy tissue in the throat that are called vocal chords. They vibrate when air passes through them, causing the sounds we call speech. The bump you touched is called the larynx. There are muscles around the larynx that determine the pitch of your speech. Can you make your voice go really high or really low? What does that feel like?

YOUR NOTES

Try lighting two candles. How hard do you have to hit the drum to blow them both out?

Try using a bigger or a smaller tube. Are your results any different?

Near or Far

Depth perception is the ability to judge how near or far objects are. What can change depth perception? Figure out the Vowel code to get directions for a simple test to help you learn more!

IN EACH HAND HOLD A PENCIL SIDEWAYS. CLOSE ONE EYE AND TRY TO TOUCH THE ERASERS TOGETHER. NEXT, TRY IT WITH BOTH EYES OPEN!

Funny Bones

You will need to break three different codes to get the answers to these wacky riddles!

Ipx epft b tdjfoujtu

hfu gsfti csfbui?

Xjui bo fyqfsj-njou!

• Letter Shift code (B=A, C=B, D=C, etc.)

Hew de yei tirn o nesu

ante o feet? Moku at twulvu

anchus leng!

• Vowel Scramble code

owH od ouy hangec yese ntoi

omethings lsee? utC na niono.

tI illw akem oury yese aterw!

• Last-to-First code

Your Skin

What is one of the most amazing organs in your body? Here are some clues: it keeps you dry, safe, and healthy. And it warms up and cools down all by itself. If you guessed your skin, you're right! Humans all pretty much have the same skin—it's made of all the same molecules and it performs the same functions. It covers our bones and muscles and tissues and organs.

But animals and birds have completely different kinds of skin. Some animals, like polar bears, have dense fur that keeps them warm in cold climates. Other animals have no hair, such as Chihuahuas and seals. Chihuahuas live in warm climates, and seals have layers of fat called blubber that keep them warm in cold ocean water. Fish have scaly skin that helps them move through water. Birds have feathers that are specially designed to help them fly.

TRY THIS
FEET FEELERS

Humans have incredibly sensitive skin, especially on our feet. Unless you walk around outside in bare feet all the time, the soles of your feet are quite soft. In this experiment, you'll rely on that sensitivity to give you clues about the things around you.

QUESTION

How does your skin help you recognize your world?

WHAT YOU NEED

Friend
Various objects with different textures, such as flannel, sandpaper, wool, Styrofoam, tape, towel, saucepan, ice cube, and so on

Super Skin

Did you know that your skin is the largest organ in your body? Full of oils and glands and layers upon layers of cells, it protects and covers your insides. Give yourself, and your skin, a big hug!

WHAT TO DO

1. Close your eyes. Have your friend place different items on the floor throughout the room.
2. Ask your friend to lead you around the room.
3. Step gently and try to identify the things you feel with your feet. Are you correct?
4. Switch with your friend. How many things did he guess correctly?
5. If you have a grassy backyard, try walking around outside. What can you feel under your feet?

WHAT'S HAPPENING

The skin is the largest organ in the human body and is made up of two layers. The outer layer is called the *epidermis*, and the inner layer is the *dermis*. The dermis has certain areas on it, called *receptors*, that send messages to the brain whenever the skin is cold or hot, wet or dry, smooth or rough.

There are certain areas on your body that are covered in hair. The hairs protect your skin from sun exposure and cold. When skin does get cold, tiny raised areas can appear, called goose bumps. They make the hairs on the skin stand up. Goose bumps can also appear when you're frightened. The action that causes goose bumps is called the *pilomotor reflex* and it is similar to a porcupine raising its quills when it's threatened.

YOUR NOTES

Which textures were easy to identify?
Which were difficult?

FUN FACT

Bones

When you were a kid, you had 300 bones in your body. But as you get older, some bones will fuse together. So when you become an adult, you will have 206 bones in your body.

TRY THIS
SKIN IS COOL!

What feels better on a hot day than a breeze? You instantly feel calmer, cooler, and happier. But are you actually cooler? Has your body temperature changed at all?

QUESTION

When it's hot outside, how does your body stay cool?

WHAT YOU NEED

A warm day
A fan
A household thermometer

WHAT TO DO

1. On a warm day, use the thermometer to tell you what the temperature is in the room. Write the temperature in the following Your Notes section.
2. How do you feel? Warm? Very warm? Write how you feel in the Your Notes section.
3. Now turn on the fan and point it at you. Do you feel cooler? Write how cool you feel in the Your Notes section.
4. Take the temperature of the room with the fan blowing. Has the temperature gone down at all? Why do you feel cooler?

WHAT'S HAPPENING

All over your skin are tiny holes called pores. If your body temperature rises above 98.6°F, glands under your skin release a liquid called sweat that seeps through your pores and out onto

Shedding Skin

When you become an adult, you will have more than 20 square feet of skin on your body. And you will have shed more than 40 pounds of skin! Ew!

the skin. This process is called perspiration. Blowing air from the fan evaporates the sweat, turning the liquid into vapor. Even if the temperature of the room doesn't change, your body is cooling down, which makes you feel better!

Your body makes more than ten ounces of sweat a day, even in winter. It's important, though, to drink lots of water, even if you're feeling cool. Your body loses moisture through perspiration and you have to stay hydrated.

Plants have their own way of releasing moisture, though it's not called perspiration, and it's not because they're hot. Plants sometimes absorb too much moisture from the ground, and so they release the water as vapor through tiny holes in their leaves called stomata. The process is called transpiration.

WORDS to KNOW

evaporation: the process by which a liquid changes into a vapor.

YOUR NOTES

Room temperature: _____

_____

How you feel before using the fan: _____

_____

_____

How you feel after using the fan: _____

_____

_____

_____

SCIENCE LAB: CAUGHT IN THE ACT

When police officers are trying to solve a crime, they look for fingerprints. In this experiment, you will gather fingerprints from your family members, your friends, and yourself and look at the prints closely. Now that's some good police work!

QUESTION

How does your fingerprint identify you?

WHAT YOU NEED

Pencil (try not to use a mechanical pencil, use a wooden one instead)
3 sheets of white paper
Rubber gloves
Transparent tape
Family members and friends
Magnifying glass

WHAT TO DO

1. Tear off several short pieces of tape. Hang the tape strips off the end of a table so that you have them handy.
2. Put a rubber glove on one hand. You'll use this hand to pick up the strips of tape. That way you won't leave a stray print on the tape.
3. Use the pencil to shade a small square on the paper. Press a little with the pencil to make sure you have a solid dark area.
4. Press your index finger into the shaded area.
5. Holding a strip of tape in your gloved hand, press your index finger into the middle of the sticky side of the tape.
6. Stick the tape to the second sheet of white paper. Label the tape "My Index Finger."
7. Print as many fingers as you like.
8. Find some family members or friends and print them, too.
9. Now that you have your fingerprints, look at them under the magnifying glass. Compare the different prints. What do you see?

WHAT'S HAPPENING

Your skin has natural oils on it that keep the skin smooth and healthy. When you touch something, you leave behind an oily impression of your skin on the object. That impression is a fingerprint. Skin is extremely flexible and elastic so it can move and stretch in all kinds of ways. As a result, no two fingerprints are exactly alike. Even identical twins will not have exactly the same prints.

Fingerprints are made up of three basic parts known as whorls, arches, and loops. Nowadays, prints are entered into a computer database to make it easier to search a print. But once upon a time, prints were identified by hand. Detectives would use the loops, whorls, and arches to figure out the owner of a fingerprint.

dactyloscopy: fingerprint identification.

YOUR NOTES

Draw a picture of the most unusual fingerprint. Who does it belong to?

Tick Tock

You can watch your heart beat without having to look at your heart!

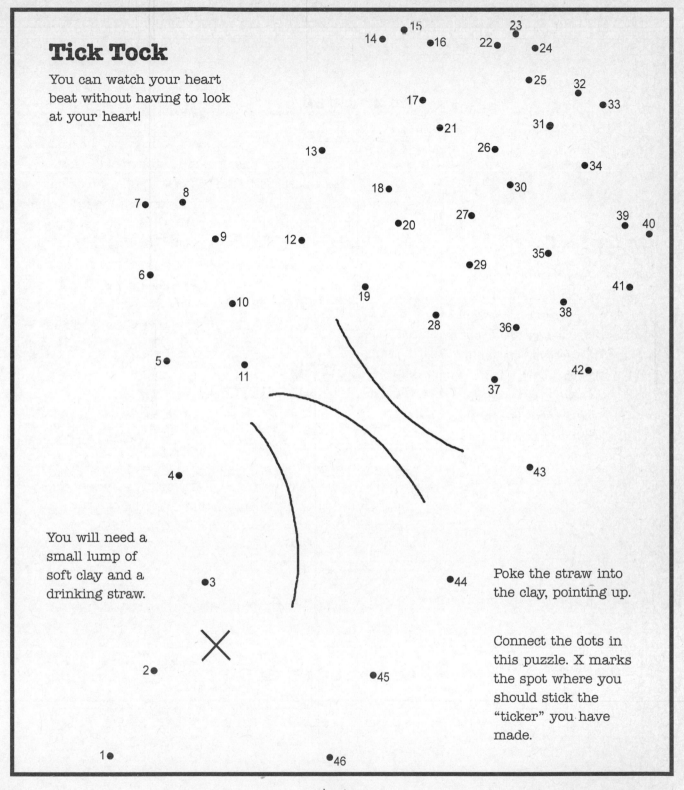

You will need a small lump of soft clay and a drinking straw.

Poke the straw into the clay, pointing up.

Connect the dots in this puzzle. X marks the spot where you should stick the "ticker" you have made.

Your Eyes

Have you ever looked closely at your eyes? The colored part is called the iris. It can be brown, blue, black, or hazel. The black part inside the iris is the pupil, which can enlarge to let in light and contract to block out too much light. There are parts of the eye you can't see, too. There is a curved and transparent part that sits in front of the iris called the cornea. Another transparent section that sits behind the pupil is called the lens. Light moves through the lens and then through a jelly contained in the eye, all the way to the retina. From there, receptors tell the brain what colors the eye is seeing.

TRY THIS
COLOR GO ROUND

Our world is incredibly colorful. From a brilliant blue sky to a crimson sports car, almost everyone sees the vast spectrum of color around us. What are your favorite colors? Which ones do you like to wear? Do you like certain foods because of their color? Or do you think about certain colors when your mood changes?

QUESTION

Why do colors seem to run together when you see them go by quickly?

WHAT YOU NEED

Small plate
Piece of cardboard
Small screw
Pen

Red marker
Blue marker
Scissors
Hole punch

FUN FACT

Do You See Color?

Different animals see different amounts of color. Dogs and cats can see some colors. Whales, sea lions, and dolphins are colorblind, meaning they see only light and dark, not colors. Monkeys and apes see as many colors as we do. And owls can see at night—some scientists even think owls can see colors in the dark!

WORDS to KNOW

colorblindness: inability to see one or more colors.

WHAT TO DO

1. Turn the plate over and place it over the cardboard.
2. Trace a circle around the plate on the cardboard.
3. Cut out the circle. Ask a grownup to punch a hole in the center of the circle.
4. Draw four straight lines across the circle, cutting it into eight sections.
5. Color one section red.
6. Color the next section blue. Continue alternating the colors around the circle.
7. Place the screw in the hole in the center of the circle.
8. Holding the screw, gently spin the circle. What happens?
9. Turn the circle over and use two new colors, like red and yellow. What do you see?
10. Make another circle and color it yellow and blue. Try the experiment again.

WHAT'S HAPPENING

When you spin the wheel quickly, your brain cannot distinguish each color. So it sees a mixture of the two colors. A wheel with red and yellow sections looks orange. A wheel with red and blue sections looks purple.

Red, yellow, and blue are called primary colors. They are used to make the secondary colors of orange, green, and purple. Color wheels also display pairs of complementary colors, which, when mixed properly, yield a bland color like white, black, or gray.

Some people experience colorblindness. While they're not technically blind, they do have trouble seeing certain colors. This can be caused by damage to the eye or the brain, or it can be genetic, which means the person inherited it from the parents. Some people who are colorblind have difficulty telling the

Mirage

Have you ever looked down a road in summer and seen a shimmer? Your eyes are playing tricks on you. It looks like there's water on the road, but in reality there's nothing there. This phenomenon is known as a mirage.

Blinkathon

The human eye blinks more than 4 million times in one year!

Ghost Nose

Here's an easy trick to play on your brain! Follow the directions to learn how to find your own ghost nose.

of
16

middle
3

and
2

tip
9

along
17

Rub
13

nose.
14

gap
8

fingers.
7

Read the numbered words in this order:

10, 4,

11, 2,

3, 7,

13, 1,

8, 6,

4, 12,

7, 17,

1, 5,

2, 15,

1, 9,

16, 4,

14

index
11

your
4

between
6

ridge
5

the
1

around
15

Cross
10

crossed
12

difference between red and green. Others have trouble with blue and yellow. And still others cannot see any color. Imagine what that must be like.

YOUR NOTES

Red and blue make _____
Red and yellow make _____
Yellow and blue make _____

TRY THIS
BUSY BOOK

Nowadays, cartoon animation is often done by a computer program, which uses math to manipulate images in a way that creates a picture that looks so realistic it's hard to tell it's a cartoon. But once upon a time, people sat and drew images and then filmed them to give the illusion of movement and life.

QUESTION

How do you make a still image move?

WHAT YOU NEED

10 square sheets of paper
Pencil
Stapler

94

WHAT TO DO

1. Line up the squares of paper so they're even.
2. Staple one side at the top and bottom to hold the sheets together. You may want to ask a grownup to help you.
3. On the first page, draw a picture of a person.
4. On the next right-hand page, draw the same person starting to take a step.
5. On the following right-hand page, draw the person taking another step. Make sure each new drawing is just a little bit different from the one before it.
6. When you have filled up the pages with drawings, close the book.
7. Then grab the stapled end in your left hand and the lower right corner with your right thumb and forefinger.
8. Carefully flip through the book. What do you see?

WHAT'S HAPPENING

If you flip through the book slowly, your eye can detect the individual images. But when you flip quickly, your eye cannot keep up, and the images seem to "move" on their own. This is a similar effect to the color wheel experiment at the beginning of this section.

When you watch TV or a movie, you are watching a series of still images scrolling at a very fast speed to trick your eye into believing the images are actually moving. It's important to remember when you're drawing these kinds of movements, however, to make your changes slight and minimal but numerous so that the motion can appear as seamless as possible.

YOUR NOTES

What other images could you draw in a flip book? Perhaps a flower opening or a caterpillar turning into a butterfly?

What did the left eye
say to the right eye?

Between you and me,
something smells!

SCIENCE LAB:
MEMORY TEST

Have you ever played a card game called Concentration? Grab a friend and lay out the entire deck of cards face down on the floor in front of you. Turn over a pair of cards. Try and remember what you've seen and where you saw them. Flip them back over. Now it's your friend's turn. Can she remember the cards you turned over and hers as well?

QUESTION

How well do you remember what you see around you?

WHAT YOU NEED

3 sheets of paper
Pencil
Tray
Ordinary objects, such as utensils, paper
    clips, scissors, ruler, stapler, bottle cap,
    and hairbrush
Stopwatch

WHAT TO DO

1. Have a grownup write some words on a sheet of paper while you look away.
2. Now look at the words for just 30 seconds. Then turn the paper over and try to recite the words from memory.
3. Check to see how you did. Record your results in the following Your Notes section.
4. Now have your partner arrange the objects you've gathered in a tray while you look away.
5. Look at the tray for 30 seconds. Close your eyes and try to recite the objects.
6. How did you do? Record your results in the Your Notes section.
7. For the last part of the experiment, have your partner make up a six-digit number and write it on the last sheet of paper. Don't look until your partner is done.
8. Take only 15 seconds this time to try to memorize the number. When time is up, look away and try to repeat it back. How did you do?
9. Now ask the grownup to try these exercises. Which of you has the better memory?

WHAT'S HAPPENING

Your brain is an incredible machine. One particular part of your brain is called the *cerebral cortex*. It handles signals from your senses. It is also in charge of helping you think and remember.

There are four kinds of memory:

- Short-term memory is used to remember a name you just heard
- Long-term memory allows you to remember something that happened years ago
- Episodic memory means you remember everything about an event, including sensory experiences
- Factual memory refers to memorizing facts and statistics

Your short-term memory is what allows you to do the previous experiment.

Starting when you are about three years old, your brain starts making memories of your experiences and actions. As you get older, you lose some memories. This is natural—the brain has to make room for new ones. But some people lose too many of their memories and it becomes hard for them to function. This is why many people work on their memory, testing it with exercises like the ones you just did, to keep their brains sharp and alert.

YOUR NOTES

Number of words you remembered:

_____

Number of objects you remembered:

_____

Numbers you remembered:

_____

Chapter 5

Planet Earth: From Deep Oceans to Our Faraway Atmosphere

Weather

Rain, snow, sleet, clouds . . . our planet has lots of different kinds of weather. Scientists who study atmosphere and weather are called *meteorologists*. You can be a meteorologist, too, with your very own rain gauge and weather vane.

TRY THIS
RAIN, RAIN GO AWAY . . .

Rainy days can be a bummer—it's not much fun to get wet and cold. You could stay inside and do some of these science experiments. Or you can turn the rainy day into an experiment!

QUESTION

How do you measure rainfall?

WHAT YOU NEED

Large jar
Ruler
Marker

WHAT TO DO

1. On the next rainy day, get a large jar and put it outside. Make sure you choose a jar that can hold a lot of water.
2. When it stops raining, bring the jar inside. Dry it off and put your ruler inside the jar.
3. Using your marker, make a line on the ruler at the level of the water.

4. Take out your ruler and look at the mark you made. That is the amount of rain that fell during the shower. Was it a light sprinkle or a heavy downpour?

WHAT'S HAPPENING

You just made your very own rain gauge. Meteorologists use rain gauges to measure rainfall in an area to better understand that area's climate. Meteorologists ask questions like, "Is this area receiving more rain than usual? Less rain?" In areas that aren't receiving enough rain, sometimes a drought alert is set. A drought is a period without any rain or insufficient rain. In areas with a lot of rain, sometimes flooding is a problem if there aren't enough drains to send the water into sewers. Later you'll see how you can use extra rainwater and conserve your use of freshwater.

WORDS to KNOW

climate: the average pattern of weather in a certain area.

We know rain comes from clouds, which are large masses of water droplets. What kinds of clouds are there in the sky? Look up into the sky. Do you see thin clouds that look like hairs? You're seeing cirrus clouds. Are the clouds puffy and piled up? Then you're seeing cumulus clouds. Cumulus clouds can occur high in the sky or closer to the ground. High cumulus clouds are small, about the size of your thumb if you hold your arm straight out. Low cumulus clouds are closer to the size of your fist. Some clouds have very unique shapes. Lenticular clouds look like a disc floating in the air. You can see them sometimes on mountaintops. Clouds can also tell you what the weather is going to be. Cumulonimbus clouds indicate bad weather.

YOUR NOTES

Use the following chart to measure rainfall over a week. See how your number increases or decreases from one day to the next. Try this at different times of the year, as well.

Monday _____

Tuesday _____

Wednesday _____

Thursday _____

Friday _____

Saturday _____

Sunday _____

Making Music

A seismologist is a scientist who studies earthquakes. What do you think a seismologist's favorite kind of music is? To find the answer, color in all the shapes that contain the letters Q, U, A, K, E.

TRY THIS
HOMEMADE RAINBOW

With clouds and rain, and a little sun, comes a rainbow! But the following experiment will show you that you don't have to wait for a gray day to see this colorful wonder!

QUESTION

How do you make a rainbow?

WHAT YOU NEED

Flat pan
Small mirror
Sunny day
White wall

WHAT TO DO

1. Fill the pan halfway with water.
2. Put the mirror up against one edge of the pan. Make sure the mirror is half in and half out of the water.
3. Set the pan by a window. Pick a window that is near a white wall.
4. Angle the pan so that the sunlight reflects off the mirror onto the wall.
5. Look at your wall. What do you see? You might have to move the pan around a little bit to get just the right angle.

WHAT'S HAPPENING

Sunlight is made up of rays. Those rays shine onto the mirror in the pan. But half of the mirror is underwater. The water breaks up the light rays into a prism of individual colors that

Cool Quotes

The universe is full of magical things patiently waiting for our wits to grow sharper.

—Eden Phillpotts

FUN FACT

Thunderstorm Countdown!

Next time there's a thunderstorm, watch for a flash of lightning. Then count slowly until you hear the thunder boom again—one-one-thousand, two-one-thousand, three-one-thousand . . . and so on. Divide the number you get by five. That's how many miles away the storm is.

WORDS to KNOW

rainbow: an arc that shows off the colors present in sunlight as it passes through water drops.

What does the Sun put in her hair in the morning?

A rain-bow!

FUN FACT

Moonbows

Some rainbows occur after the sun has set! A full moon shines bright light through a rainfall or a waterfall. This causes a dim moonbow to appear in the sky. You can see moonbows in many places, including Hawaii and Victoria Falls in Africa.

make up sunlight. Those colorful rays appear on the wall as a rainbow. When you see a rainbow in the sky, sunlight is passing through raindrops at an angle that allows you to see the colors in light.

The prism of colors includes red, orange, yellow, green, blue, indigo, and violet. You can see rainbows in mist from a waterfall, dewdrops on a web, and an oily puddle on the street. Anyplace where light rays hit water at just the right angle, you can see that prism. The best thing to do on a day when it's raining and it's sunny is to stand with your back to the sunlight. Then look up into the sky. Chances are, if you're patient, you'll find a rainbow. You might even find two. Double bows are not uncommon. The arc is cut by the horizon, but if you're up in a plane, you just might see the whole circle!

YOUR NOTES

Draw a picture of your rainbow.

Rain in a Jar

With just a few simple ingredients, you can make a rainstorm in a jar! You will need a large clear jar with a metal lid, several ice cubes, and some very hot water. Follow the directions to color in the puzzle grid and see how to put your rain jar together. Have an adult help with the very hot water, please!

J = GRAY
(this is the jar)

L = BLACK
(this is the lid)

W = DARK BLUE
(this is the hot water)

R = LIGHT BLUE
(this is the rain)

I = WHITE
(this is the ice)

A = WHITE
(this is air)

B = YELLOW
(this is the background)

```
B B B B B B B B B B B B B B B B
B B B B B B B B I I I B B B B B
B B B B B B B B I I I B B B B B
B B B B I I I B I I I B B B B B
B B B B I I I B B B B B B B B B
B B B L I I I B B B B L B B B
B B B L L L L L L L L L B B B
B B B J I R I R I R I J B B B
B B B J I I I I I I I J B B B
B B B J I R I I I R I J B B B
B B J I I I I I I I I J B B
B J I I I I R I I I I I J B
B J I I I R I I I R I I I J B
B J I I I I I R I I I I I J B
B J I I I I I I I I I I I J B
B J I I I R I I I R I I I J B
B J I I I I I I I I I I I J B
B J I I I I I R I I I I I J B
B J I I I R I I I I I I I J B
B J I I I I I I I I I I I J B
B J I I I I I I I R I I I J B
B J I I I I I I I I I I I J B
B J I I I I I I I I I I I J B
B J W W W W W W W W W W W J B
B J W W W W W W W W W W W J B
B J W W W W W W W W W W W J B
B B J J J J J J J J J J J B B
B B B B B B B B B B B B B B B B
```

SCIENCE LAB: WEATHER VANE

Weather vanes come in all shapes and sizes. Sometimes they have roosters, sometimes other animals, or even people. Some are fancy and ornamental. Others are simply designed. But almost all have arrows and compass directions. And they are all blown about by high winds and gentle breezes.

QUESTION

How do you know which way the wind is blowing?

WHAT YOU NEED

Cardboard (You could use an old milk carton)
Ruler
Pencil
Scissors
Pin
Dime or a nickel
Tape
Sewing thread (about a foot long)
Windy day

WHAT TO DO

1. Draw an arrow on the cardboard and cut it out carefully.
2. Tear off a piece of tape and attach the coin to the tip of the arrow.
3. Now hold the middle of the arrow with two fingers. Does the arrow tip forward or backward?
4. Slide your fingers toward the front or the back of the arrow until it doesn't tip anymore. The spot where you're holding the arrow is the balance point. Mark that point with your pencil.
5. Put the pin through the mark, close to the top edge of the arrow.
6. Hold the arrow by the pin to double check that the arrow is balanced.
7. Remove the pin and slip the thread through the hole, tying a knot.
8. Now you have a weather vane. Take it outside and hold the other end in one hand. Stretch your arm out straight so the arrow won't hit your body.
9. As the wind blows, watch the weather vane. How does it move?

WHAT'S HAPPENING

Weather vanes are used to see where the wind is coming from. This helps meteorologists understand weather patterns. The tip of the arrow points in the direction the wind is blowing. Wind direction is the opposite of where the arrow is pointing. The flat end of the arrow will move even in a light breeze.

Weather vanes are often found on top of houses and high up on buildings. That way they can blow about and not hit anything like tree branches or power lines. Also, the wind is more likely to blow in one direction up high. Closer to the ground, the wind can change direction constantly.

A windsock is another kind of weather vane. You can see windsocks at airports. They are used to indicate wind direction and approximate wind speed. Airports worry about these things because of the risk of a gasoline leak. Windsocks are often illuminated so that readings can be taken at night.

YOUR NOTES

Try making arrows out of thin paper and thick cardboard. Do they work better in light breezes or heavy winds?

Decorate your weather vane and attach it somewhere outside. Take a look at it each day to see which direction the winds are blowing.

Active Earth

Earth is an active planet that is constantly reshaping itself. Huge mountains of ice are melting from changes in the climate. Unique animals live in deep-sea vents, braving acidic water, high pressure, and more. Winds swirl and blast across farmlands, flattening crops and blowing through towns. Through the following experiments, we can better understand these natural events.

10. MOUTH   2. ROOM   9. SAVERS   12. OPEN

5. WINT   7. GREEN

1. DARK   11. CHEW

Sweet Lightning

Make tiny sparks of lightning and have a sweet treat at the same time! Use the numbered words to fill in the blanks and learn how.

Go into a _____ _____ . Look in a _____
　　　　　　1　　　2　　　　　　　　3
while you _____ several _____ - _ - _____
　　　　　　　4　　　　　　　5　　6　　7
_____ in your _____ . Be sure to
　8　　　9　　　　　10
_____ with your _____ _____ .
　11　　　　　　　10　　　12

8. LIFE   4. CRUNCH   6. O   3. MIRROR

108

 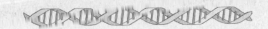

TRY THIS
ICEBERG!

An iceberg is a chunk of frozen freshwater that has broken off of a larger glacier or ice shelf and is floating out in open water. Icebergs may not look very big above the surface of the water, but they can extend deep underwater. This is what makes them dangerous to boats. It may be difficult to see the floating part of the iceberg, and so the boat can run into the lower section and crash.

QUESTION

If all the oceans' icebergs melt, would the seas flood and drown the land?

WHAT YOU NEED

Drinking glass
6 to 8 ice cubes
Warm water

WHAT TO DO

1. Pour the ice cubes into the glass.
2. Make a prediction. What do you think will happen when you fill the glass with warm water?
3. Now pour the water into the glass.
4. Was your prediction right?

WHAT'S HAPPENING

Did you think the water would overflow the glass? Were you surprised when it didn't? The melting ice cubes don't take up more space in the glass, they simply move the water aside.

WORDS to KNOW

iceberg: large, floating chunk of freshwater ice that broke off of a larger glacier.

FUN FACT

Pop! Fizz!

When an iceberg melts, air bubbles are trapped in the snow layers. When the bubbles pop, the iceberg makes a fizzing sound.

They have the same mass as they did when they were cubes. So the level of the water will not change.

Icebergs in the ocean act the same way. As icebergs melt, they take up the same space in the water, so they will not cause the seas to overflow. Glaciers on land, however, will significantly raise water levels in the world's seas if they all melt.

Icebergs come in different shapes. A dome is an iceberg whose top is rounded. An iceberg called a pinnacle has spires on top. If you see an iceberg with a steep cliff and a slope, it's called a wedge.

YOUR NOTES

Look up the tallest iceberg in the world. Then measure your height. How many of you does it take to make up the tallest iceberg?

TRY THIS
TWIRLING TORNADO

In the United States, tornadoes seem to mostly occur in the spring down south and in the summer up north. While tornadoes can hit at any time of day, they seem to usually start in the late afternoon and evening. The winds typically move from southwest to northeast.

QUESTION

How do tornadoes move?

What is a tornado's favorite dance?

The twist!

FUN FACT

Tornado Alley

While tornadoes happen all over the world, most twisters touch down in the midwestern United States. Three out of four tornadoes in the world occur in the central states, earning this area the nickname Tornado Alley.

WHAT YOU NEED

2 clear and clean 2-liter plastic soda bottles
Water
Washer
Duct tape

FUN FACT

The Rumbling Earth

Although big earthquakes can be dangerous, most earthquakes are small and barely felt by people.

WHAT TO DO

1. Fill the first bottle ⅔ full of water.
2. Place the washer on the opening of the first bottle.
3. Place the second bottle upside-down on top of the washer, so the openings are touching each other.
4. Tear off a strip of duct tape and carefully wrap it around the necks of the bottles, making sure the bottles are straight up and down. We don't want any water to leak out.
5. Flip the bottles over so that the bottle with the water is on top.
6. Move the bottles rapidly in a circle.
7. What do you see in the top bottle?

WHAT'S HAPPENING

When you swirled the bottles you created a spinning flow of water, called a *vortex*, which imitated a tornado. Tornadoes are funnel-shaped winds that twist and blow at speeds of 200 to 300 miles an hour over mostly flat land. Twisters usually only last a few minutes, but they can cause a lot of damage.

Our Earth is surrounded by a layer of air, called the *atmosphere*, that is constantly changing. Our weather takes place in the troposphere, an area of the

You Got the Whole World in Your Hand

Here is a simple description of the Earth's layers:

CRUST — The outer layer is thin. It can be easily cracked and moved.

MANTLE — The middle layer is thick and firm but slippery.

CORE — The very center of the Earth is a small, hot sphere.

Can you think of an object that fits this description and is small enough to fit in your hand?

If you need a hint, look at the paragraph below in a mirror.

THIS COMMON BREAKFAST FOOD COMES FROM A CHICKEN AND IS COOKED IN BOILING WATER

atmosphere that is closest to the Earth. So what's happening when a tornado forms? Winds suddenly change direction, moving faster and higher, spinning through the atmosphere. A thunderstorm builds in the sky, and rising air from the ground pushes the spinning winds up toward the storm. Eventually the air turns into a vertical funnel, carrying with it dust, debris, hail, and punishing winds.

YOUR NOTES

Twister alert! If there's a threat of a twister in your area, there will be an emergency broadcast on the TV or on the radio giving you information about what to do. A Tornado Watch means that there could be tornadoes in your area. Watch for any storms. A Tornado Warning indicates that the weather service has spotted a tornado. Thunderstorm Warnings are issued when severe thunderstorms are coming. Make sure you know where to go and what to do in case of a bad storm

SCIENCE LAB:
DEEP-SEA VOLCANO

Did you know volcanoes can occur underwater? Did you know there are mountain chains underwater, too? The mid-ocean ridge is the longest mountain chain on Earth—it is 40,000 miles long! And it has hydrothermal vents that spew extremely hot water up into the cold ocean. These vents are located more than 12,000 feet below the surface of the ocean. The water from these vents is full of minerals and bacteria that, at a temperature of 750°F, combine to create an extreme environment in which certain organisms thrive.

QUESTION

What causes underwater volcanoes?

WHAT YOU NEED

Adult
Small plastic bottle with a narrow opening
Kitchen tongs
Large plastic jar with a wide opening
Hot and cold water
Food coloring

WHAT TO DO

1. Make sure the small bottle fits completely inside the large jar.
2. Pour cold water into the large jar so that it is three-quarters full.
3. Ask an adult to heat some water. The water should be hot but not boiling.
4. Have the adult pour the hot water into the small bottle and use the tongs to put the bottle into the jar. The bottle should sit below the water level in the jar.
5. Add some food coloring to the water. What do you see?

WHAT'S HAPPENING

Hot water is less dense and lighter than cold water. So in this experiment, when the hot water in the bottle hit the cold water in the jar, the hot water rushed up to the surface, creating a small volcano.

Our planet is made up of a hot molten core, a thick mantle that surrounds the core, and a thin crust of rock plates that covers the mantle. The plates form our continents and oceans. Heat and pressure from the core boil up and cause the plates to move and shift, leading to earthquakes and volcanoes. Molten rock from the core meets frigid seawater, cooling to form mountain ranges such as the mid-ocean ridge.

Cracks in the mountains allow cold seawater to flood down to the core, where it is heated to extreme temperatures. Because hot water is less dense than cold water, as we saw in the previous experiment, the now-boiling seawater bubbles back up through these hydrothermal vents and we have an undersea eruption. Some of these vents are several stories tall!

Who could possibly live near these sweltering, acidic vents? Many of the species that live in this climate are brand new to scientists, who have only recently started exploring this area of the ocean. There are bacteria, shrimplike creatures, tubeworms, mussels, clams, and many others.

YOUR NOTES

Do the experiment again and try mixing food coloring to see what happens.

Draw your deep-sea volcano here.

FUN FACT

Go Diving!

The Great Barrier Reef in Australia is the largest coral reef on Earth and the biggest living construction made up of tiny organisms. The reef is about 1,600 miles long.

Why did the ocean wave?

It wanted to say hello.

Protecting the Earth

Our planet is an amazing place, filled with living seas, towering mountains, and incredible wildlife. But we need to take better care of our world. Every day, we do things that harm the environment. We burn too much coal and oil, which produces harmful gases. These gases rise up into our atmosphere and cause global problems. We scrape away too much rock from our mountains to harvest minerals. We cut down too many trees in our already dwindling forests. We send out fleets of fishing boats that comb the seas for more and more fish.

These are big problems that we can all try and change through the decisions we make every day. These decisions can help improve things for the future. Try the following experiments to learn what is happening to the Earth and what you can do to help.

TRY THIS
A GREENHOUSE IN A BOX

Life on Earth is possible because of energy from the sun. The sun radiates, or gives off its energy in the form of heat and light that travel in waves, like the ones you made with a ribbon earlier in the book. The sun's energy is very hot and very bright. But all objects radiate some amount of heat and light. A radiator, for instance, warms up a cold room and a light bulb illuminates a dark room.

Greenhouse gases, including water vapor, carbon dioxide, methane, nitrous oxide, and ozone, exist to absorb the Sun's radiation, sending heat both up into space and down onto the Earth's surface, protecting the Earth. But what happens when the gases can't send that heat out into space and it gets trapped?

Stinky Cows

Cows do more than moo as they stand in the fields and chew their cud. They burp and fart a gas called methane. This gas is one of the many greenhouse gases that are damaging the Earth's atmosphere. In one day the average cow will let loose dozens of gallons of gas. Pee-yoo!

greenhouse: a glass-enclosed building used to grow plants.

QUESTION

What is the greenhouse effect?

WHAT YOU NEED

Shoebox with lid removed
Small bag of soil
2 thermometers
Clear plastic wrap
Stopwatch
Pen

Cool Quotes

We do not inherit the earth from our ancestors, we borrow it from our children.

—Native American proverb

WHAT TO DO

1. Ready to get your hands dirty? Dig into the bag and dump handfuls of dirt into the shoebox so that the box is about half full.
2. Put one thermometer on top of the bed of soil.
3. Wrap the shoebox in plastic wrap.
4. Put the shoebox in a sunny place and set the second thermometer next to the box.
5. Read the temperatures on both thermometers and record the numbers in the following Your Notes section. Start your stopwatch.
6. Wait 15 minutes. Read the temperatures again. Mark the numbers under the Second Reading column in your table.
7. Keep reading and marking the temperatures every fifteen minutes for an hour. What are you noticing about the temperature inside the box?

WHAT'S HAPPENING

You have made a greenhouse. A green-house is a glass building used to grow plants. Sunlight shines through the glass, warms the building, and gives plants the light they need to grow. Sunlight contains heat, and it raises the temperature inside the green-house. The plastic wrap on your box acts like the glass on a green-house, holding in sun-light and raising the temperature inside the box.

Our atmosphere contains some of the heat from the sun to keep Earth's temperature livable. But now the atmosphere is full of dangerous levels of the greenhouse gases, and they are trapping too much sunlight and heat rather than letting them escape into space. As the Earth's temperature rises, polar ice caps melt, our weather undergoes significant changes, and our environment suffers.

YOUR NOTES

Temperature	Initial Reading	Second Reading	Third Reading	Fourth Reading
Inside				
Outside				

The Answer Is "Endless Number of Times!"

What is the question?

To find out, use a light-colored marker to connect the letters.

Follow these directions:

— Begin in the square below the word "START."

— Follow the arrows.

— If a square has no arrow, keep going in the same direction until you find the next arrow.

Extra Fun:

Read the unused letters in order from left to right and top to bottom to find a fun recycling fact!

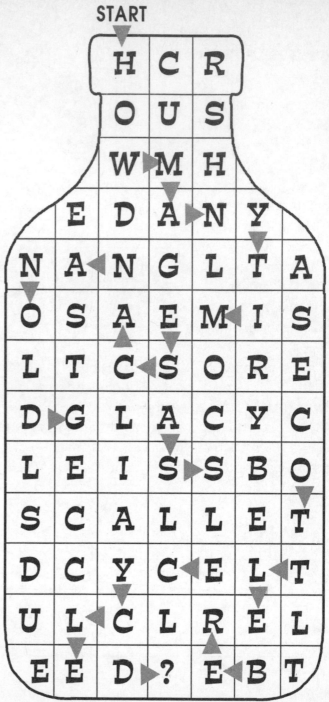

START

OUR ATMOSPHERE IN A JAR

Here is a similar kind of experiment to A Greenhouse in a Box but with a slightly different approach.

QUESTION

What is happening to our atmosphere as the temperature of our planet rises?

WHAT YOU NEED

Small glass jar with lid   Sunny spot outdoors
1 teaspoon water

WHAT TO DO

1. Pour the water into the glass jar.
2. Put the lid on the jar and make sure it's tightly closed.
3. Set the jar outside in the sun for about an hour.
4. What do you see in the jar? What happened to the water?

WHAT'S HAPPENING

As the temperature of the jar warmed up from the sun's heat, the water evaporated into the air of the jar. But the vapor could not escape the jar, so it turned back into condensation in the form of droplets of water clinging to the sides of the jar. The lid on the jar acts like the plastic wrap in the last experiment, creating a greenhouse environment.

YOUR NOTES

What happens when you open the lid and let the jar sit for a bit?

atmosphere: a layer of air surrounding the planet.

Earth Day!

April 22 is Earth Day—a special day when we think about how we can take better care of our wonderful planet. But every day can be Earth Day!

TRY THIS
MAKE YOUR HOME GREEN

Now that we've seen the effects of global warming and the greenhouse problem, how can we go about changing the way we live our lives at home and in our communities to reduce our effect on the environment?

QUESTION

How green is your home?

WHAT YOU NEED

Your family
Pencil

WHAT TO DO

1. Read the list in the following Your Notes section. It explains all kinds of things you can do to help the environment.
2. With your family, use the list to see which things you're already doing and which things you can start doing.
3. Don't feel like you need to accomplish everything on the whole list all at once. Choose a few things to do at a time. It's always important to make sure you are being ecologically responsible.

WHAT'S HAPPENING

Caring for our planet begins at home. By looking around your house and changing simple things in your life, you can do your part to help conserve precious resources. Earth is a big planet with many, many people depending on the same water, food,

Cool Quotes

Take nothing but photos, leave nothing but footprints, kill nothing but time.

—Motto of the Baltimore Grotto

fuel, and air. We must think like a global community and make wise decisions based on how everyone on the planet might be affected.

YOUR NOTES

Kitchen/Bathroom

- Make sure the faucet is turned off and not dripping. Leaky faucets can waste thousands of gallons of water a year.
- Use less soap when you wash your hands or take a bath. You can still get clean and save soap. This means you won't have to buy soap as often, and you'll create less waste.
- Turn off the faucet when you're brushing and flossing your teeth.
- Wash dishes in cold or lukewarm water rather than hot water. You'll save energy and money.

Living Room/Dining Room

- Turn off the lights when you're not in the room. Electricity comes from a power plant that burns coal. A byproduct of burning coal is carbon dioxide, which is a greenhouse gas.
- Turn off the TV and the computer when you're not using them.
- Use the backs of envelopes for grocery lists or quick phone messages rather than always using a fresh sheet of paper.
- Lower the thermostat by two degrees in winter so that the heater doesn't have to work so hard to heat the house. In the summer, raise the thermostat two degrees so that the air conditioner doesn't have to work so hard.

Plant a Tree!

Trees are essential to our survival on Earth. By planting an acre of trees, we can remove more than two tons of carbon dioxide from the air.

- Throughout the house, replace your regular light bulbs with energy-saving light bulbs. You'll save money and electricity.

Your Room

- Donate toys, games, and books you no longer use so that others can use them and not have to buy new ones. Reusing and sharing existing products creates less waste.
- Donate old clothes or find ways to reuse the material to make bags or hats or scarves.
- Use rechargeable batteries so that you don't have to constantly buy new batteries.

Outside the House

- Find a large barrel to collect rainwater. Rainwater can be used to water plants in the garden, to wash the car, and to clean the floors in your house.
- Plant flowers to encourage bees to visit your garden. Bees are very important for our environment.
- Make sure the faucet to the garden hose is tightly turned off. In the winter, disconnect the hose to prevent water from freezing and bursting the hose.

Everyday Life

- Go to the library to check out books rather than always buying new books. This saves resources and money.
- Invent games to play outside rather than always turning on the TV or playing video games. Appliances use electricity, which burns our natural resources. Playing outside is healthy and fun, too!
- Walk, ride your bike, or take public transportation when you're traveling around town. Avoid driving in the car unless you're going long distances. Then see if you can carpool with some friends to save gas.

FUN FACT

The Re-Cycle

So what happens when you recycle? The first step lies with people like you who sort recyclable items into the correct bins—paper, glass, metal—so that they can be collected by the city. Next, the city does another sort and cleans the objects, getting them ready for sale to manufacturers who will use them in their products. The last step lies once again with you to buy products that are made from recycled products to keep the recycling cycle going.

- Bring reusable bags to the grocery store rather than always using plastic bags. Plastic bags do not break down in our garbage and biodegrade. Instead, they sit in our landfills for a very long time.
- Shop for locally grown produce rather than buying fruits and vegetables that come from other countries. When we import our food, we use up resources that we could save if we bought the food nearby.

SCIENCE LAB: READY TO RECYCLE

Have you looked in your garbage can recently? Phew! It's probably pretty stinky. But there may be things in there that don't need to be thrown out and could actually be recycled. Are you ready to do some icky detective work?

QUESTION

How much of our garbage could actually be recycled?

WHAT YOU NEED

Adult
Tarp
Recent trash bag
Extra trash bags
Rubber gloves
Pen

WHAT TO DO

1. Spread out the tarp on the kitchen floor. This experiment might get messy!
2. With an adult's help, dump out the garbage bag onto the tarp.
3. Put on your rubber gloves. Separate out each item in the garbage according to the table in the following Your Notes section.
4. Count how many items you have in each pile and mark the number in the table. What do you notice about your garbage and recycling piles?
5. Have an adult help you put each pile into a recycling container. Don't dump the plastic bags, though. They can't be recycled by your city. Can you think of some uses for the bags?

WHAT'S HAPPENING

Household garbage often contains many items that can actually be recycled. Some people think that they don't need to sort through their garbage. They think the city will take care of it for them. But instead, all the items just go into landfills. It is important for every person to take charge and do his or her part to reduce the amount of waste we produce.

In fact, there may be some things in your recycle pile that were already made of recycled paper. Cereal boxes, notebook paper, and other things made of cardboard are often constructed using recycled materials and fibers. So you are continuing the recycling process!

Make sure you wash your hands and the items you're going to recycle when you're done.

YOUR NOTES

Garbage	Metal	Plastic	Paper/Cardboard	Glass
Trash				
Recycling				

WORDS to KNOW

landfill: a way of taking care of a large amount of waste by burying it in the ground.

Change of Habit

This experiment will take a long time to do, but when you are finished, your family might have a new, energy-saving habit!

Complete this puzzle to get directions for the experiment. Look at the fraction below each blank. Pick the shape that shows that fraction using these rules: the white part of each shape is empty; the shaded part of each shape is full. Write the letter of that shape on the line.

F __ __ __ __ M __ __ __ __ , __ A __ G
  ⅓ ¼   ⅓ ½ ⅔   ⅓ ½ 2/4 ⅖   ⅖   ½

__ __ __ __ __ __ S __ U __ SID __ __ D __ Y.
3/6 2/6 ⅓ 2/4 ⅖ ⅔   ⅓ 2/4   ⅔ 2/4 ⅓   ¼

__ __ __ CK __ H __ __ __ __ __ __ __ __ I __ BI __ __
3/6 ⅖ ⅔   2/4   ⅔   ⅔ 2/6 ⅔ 3/6 2/4 ¼   3/6   2/6 2/6

B __ F __ __ __ A __ D AF __ __ __ .
  ⅔ ⅓ ¼ ⅔   ½   2/4 ⅔ ¼

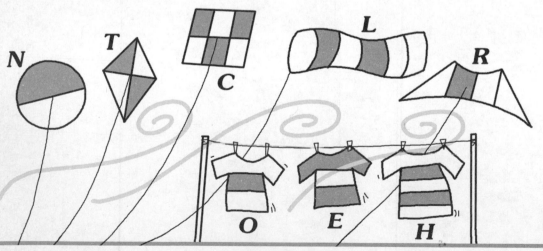

One Last Thing . . .

Now that you've tried these experiments, you may have found that some of them didn't work just right for you the first time. Sometimes you have to adjust a step, sometimes you have to make sure you're measuring correctly, and then sometimes things just don't work the way you want them to.

It's important not to give up. Many famous scientists have tried experiments that they were sure would work. They were disappointed when they didn't get any results. But they tried again and again, changing one thing or another, always thinking about how to improve their methods and ideas

Be patient, be persistent, and most importantly, have a good time. Always ask questions about everything. Look for things that other people pass by. Slow down and observe. Be a scientist and go explore the world!

Cool Quotes

This world, after all our science and sciences, is still a miracle; wonderful, inscrutable, magical and more, to whosoever will think of it.

—Thomas Carlyle

Appendix A
Glossary

acid
Something that is sour.

amplifier
Something that amplifies, or increases, current, voltage, or power.

atmosphere
A layer of air surrounding the planet.

attract
To pull toward oneself, like two magnets with opposite poles facing each other.

buoyancy
An upward force exerted on an object that is equal to the weight of the water displaced by the object.

carbon dioxide (CO_2)
A colorless, odorless gas that is found in carbonated sodas.

carnivore
An animal that eats other animals.

charge
A specific amount of electricity.

chemical change
A chemical process by which a new substance is created.

classification
The careful arrangement of information into categories.

climate
The average pattern of weather in a certain area.

colorblindness
The inability to see one or more colors.

community
A group that interacts and lives in a common area.

condensation
The process by which water changes from a gas to a liquid.

coniferous
Evergreen trees and shrubs that have needles instead of leaves.

consumer
An organism that consumes, or eats, another organism in a food chain.

dactyloscopy
Fingerprint identification.

deciduous
Trees that shed their leaves in fall and grow new ones in spring.

echo
The repetition of a sound caused by sound waves bouncing off of an object.

echolocation
Using echoes (bouncing sound waves) to determine the location of something. Bats and dolphins rely on echolocation to navigate.

ecosystem
A community of living things.

elastic
Able to be stretched and then returned to its original shape.

evaporation
The process by which liquid changes into a vapor.

frost
The layer of tiny ice crystals on a cold surface.

gait
How an animal moves.

gas
Something that has no shape or volume, like water vapor or carbon dioxide.

gravity
The force that holds objects close to the Earth's surface. On the Moon, there is no gravity, and objects just float around in space.

greenhouse
A glass-enclosed building used to grow plants.

group
A collection that shares similarities, as in a kind of classification.

habitat
The place where a plant or an animal usually lives and gets what it needs to live.

herbivore
An animal that eats only plants.

iceberg
A large, floating chunk of freshwater ice that broke off of a larger glacier.

kingdom
One of the three main divisions in biological classification.

landfill
A way of taking care of a large amount of waste by burying it in the ground.

light
Waves produced by the sun that enable us to see.

limestone
Rock formed mostly by remains of sea shells and consisting of calcium carbonate.

magnet
A mass of iron or steel or some mixture of both that can attract iron and that produces a magnetic field.

meteorologist
Someone who studies the weather.

palindrome
A word that reads the same forward and backward.

pole
One end of a magnet, either north or south.

producer
The member of the food chain that produces energy for the other members of the food chain.

protein
An essential part of the food we eat that helps our bodies grow healthy and strong.

rainbow
An arc that shows off the colors present in sunlight as it passes through water drops.

reflection
When light waves bounce back from a surface.

refraction
When light bends because it passes through a substance such as glass or water.

repel
To push away from oneself, such as two magnets with the same poles facing each other.

reproduce
To make more of something, such as plants or animals.

seed
A grain or fruit that enables a plant to reproduce itself.

sound
Vibrations transmitted through air or another medium that we can hear.

static electricity
Electricity caused by rubbing two objects together.

surface tension
The force that holds water molecules together and allows water to have a kind of skin.

transpiration
The process by which moisture is released from a plant in the form of water vapor.

vibrate
To move back and forth, or to and fro, rhythmically and rapidly.

volume
The measurement of the space taken up by an object.

water vapor
Water in the form of a gas, present in the atmosphere.

weight
The measurement of how heavy something is.

Bubbles and Butter pg. 7

L	O	O	K	⬛	A	T	⬛	A	⬛	S	L	I	C	E	⬛	O	F
B	R	E	A	D	⬛	T	H	R	O	U	G	H	⬛	A	⬛	⬛	⬛
M	A	G	N	I	F	Y	I	N	G	⬛	G	L	A	S	S	.	⬛
T	H	E	⬛	H	O	L	E	S	⬛	A	R	E	⬛	M	A	D	E
B	Y	⬛	B	U	B	B	L	E	S	⬛	O	F	⬛	G	A	S	⬛
P	R	O	D	U	C	E	D	⬛	A	S	⬛	Y	E	A	S	T	⬛
C	E	L	L	S	⬛	G	R	O	W	.	⬛	⬛	⬛	⬛	⬛	⬛	⬛

Criss-Cross pg. 10

I CROSSED A DOG WITH A BOOMERANG.

WHAT DID YOU GET?

A PET THAT RUNS AWAY, BUT ALWAYS COMES BACK!

Whirly Seeds pg. 8

Completed Whirly Seed

Diamond Poem pg. 17

Here is one way to fill in the diamond poem. Everyone's poem will be slightly different.

OCEAN
WET, SALTY
CRASHING, WAVING, SPRAYING
BOAT, FISH, SAND, LIZARD
BAKING, BLOWING, DRIFTING
HOT, DRY
DESERT

Hidden Habitat pg. 13

Food Chain pg. 18

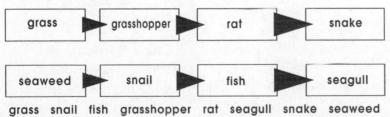

grass	▶	grasshopper	▶	rat	▶	snake

seaweed	▶	snail	▶	fish	▶	seagull

grass snail fish grasshopper rat seagull snake seaweed

Air-mazing pg. 30

> To read this code, you need to turn the page upside-down in front of a mirror.

Slice an apple. Leave it uncovered. Check it after an hour or more. The apple slice will have turned brown.

From the Piggy Bank pg. 31

```
S i O f A y K o A u F a O
r L D e E r D e P A a P d
E i R n T O g W E t L h i
s I S N e t V I N o E f l
G A e R . t L A t Y e r 3
s S H , I N y Y o u N E w
W i P E l N N l I E g S e
t O t h N e T O w P . r W
o A N I T g a 2 n 4 s w e
r H O T U R o S . t T H h
E i G R s E E p N u C z O
L O R z Y O l U e S . E E
s I S t C a O r P P t E o
R v A C e E r T A T ! E !
```

Yum-istry pg. 32

The remaining descriptions are:
— flavor must last a long time
— must feel good to chew
— must get soft but not gooey
— must not dry out in the package
— must not stick to the wrapper
— must make good-sized bubbles

This list describes BUBBLE GUM.

Way to Glow! pg. 36

D+1	W-1	G-2	N+4	X+1		V-2	H+1	H+5	5
E	V	E	R	Y		T	I	M	E
Z-1	N+1	N+7		A+2	T-2	C-2	3	C+8	
Y	O	U		C	R	A	C	K	
1	A+13	A+3		Q+2	D+4	D-3	H+3	A+4	H-7
A	N	D		S	H	A	K	E	A
M-6	M-1	15	Z-3		P+5	P+4	9	I-6	1+2
G	L	O	W		S	T	I	C	K	!

Which Is Which? pg. 38

SENSE OF SMELL

Molecules in the air have a chemical reaction with special cells in your nose. This allows you to smell the difference between the clear liquids in the three glasses.

Tasty pg. 44

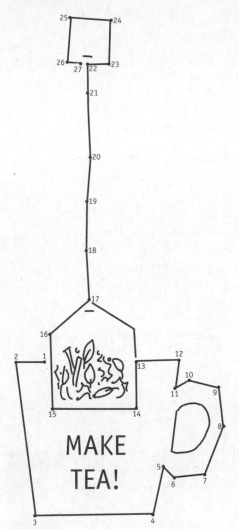

MAKE TEA!

Invisible Filler pg. 50

<u>Crumple</u> the paper.
10

<u>Stuff</u> it <u>tightly</u> deep
1   9

<u>into</u> the glass. Hold
3

the <u>glass</u> so the <u>mouth</u>
5   2

is facing <u>down</u>, and
8

push it slowly <u>into</u> the
3

<u>water</u>. Hold it there for
7

a <u>minute</u>. Carefully pull
4

the <u>glass</u> out of the
5

<u>water</u> and <u>remove</u> the
7   6

paper.

What happened? You will notice that the paper is dry when you pull it out of the glass. This is because water cannot get into the glass — the glass is already filled with air! If you tipped the glass slightly the air would bubble out, water would rush in, and the paper would get wet.

Mega Mirror pg. 52

The moon acts like a gigantic mirror. It makes no light of its own — moonlight is just sunlight bouncing off the surface of the moon!

What a Drag! pg. 55

TAKE TWO PIECES OF PAPER. CRUMPLE ONE, LEAVE ONE FLAT. TOSS THEM INTO THE AIR. ONE WILL FALL MORE SLOWLY.

There is more drag on the flat piece of paper because it has more surface area than the crumpled ball of paper.

Slo-Mo Rainbow pg. 58

~~SAMPLE~~	**POUR**	~~ONE~~	~~BET~~	*CUP*
MILK	~~GET~~	*INTO*	**A**	~~PET~~
~~SET~~	*SHALLOW*	~~COPPER~~	*BOWL.*	**WAIT**
UNTIL	**MILK**	~~IS~~	~~SALTY~~	*STILL.*
~~SADDLE~~	*CAREFULLY*	~~SAT~~	*ADD*	~~LET~~
FOOD	**COLOR**	~~POPPED~~	~~ZIPPY~~	**IN**
~~SASH~~	~~HAPPEN~~	*PATTERN*	**SHOWN.**	~~SAUCE~~
~~ADD~~	**ONE**	~~JET~~	~~TIPPED~~	~~DROP~~
~~PET~~	**OF**	*LIQUID*	~~MET~~	**SOAP**
IN	~~DRIPPY~~	~~THE~~	*MIDDLE.*	~~YET~~

What Happened: The surface tension of a liquid is caused by the attraction of the molecules to each other. The dish soap breaks the surface tension of the milk. As it spreads, it grabs the food color that is floating on top of the milk and swirls the colors together. These molecules are moving slowly. Check the bowl again in 10 minutes as see how your rainbow has changed!

Bloop pg. 59

```
B E N D J U B
S S A L G D W
L N X U K S A
Q U N S N U T
X K L A X F E
N O I L J N R
D S U T N Q U
```

Take the G L A S S.
Fill it two-thirds with
W A T E R. Pour in a
quarter inch of O I L.
Pour in an eighth of
a cup of S A L T.

What is happening? The oil is less dense than the water, so it floats on top. The heavy salt traps some oil and brings it to the bottom of the glass. As the salt dissolves, the oil BLOOPs back to the top!

Plus and Minus pg. 66

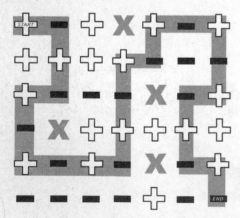

Open and Shut pg. 77

T	U	R	N		O	N		T	H	E		L	I	G	H	T
		A	N	D		L	O	O	K		I	N		T	H	E
M	I	R	R	O	R	.		H	O	W		B	I	G		A	R	E
Y	O	U	R		P	U	P	I	L	S	?		T	U	R	N
	O	F	F		T	H	E		L	I	G	H	T		A	N	D
C	O	U	N	T		T	O		2	0	.		T	U	R	N		O	N
T	H	E		L	I	G	H	T		-		Q	U	I	C	K	L	Y
L	O	O	K		A	T		Y	O	U	R		P	U	P	I	L	S	.
W	H	A	T		D	I	D		T	H	E	Y		D	O	?

What's That Sound? pg. 81

The blood surging through the veins in your ears!

Near or Far pg. 83

ANSWER: In each hand hold a sideways pencil. Close one eye and try to touch the erasers together. Next try it with both eyes open.

What's going on? Your depth perception is better when you use both eyes. That's because your brain is getting more information — it compares and combines the images from both eyes to give you a better sense of how the pencils are moving.

Funny Bones pg. 84

How does a scientist get fresh breath? With an experi-mint!

How do you turn a nose into a foot? Make it twelve inches long!

How do you change eyes into something else? Cut an onion. It will make your eyes water!

Ghost Nose pg. 94

Cross your index and middle fingers. Rub the gap between your crossed fingers along the ridge and around the tip of your nose.

Tick Tock pg. 91

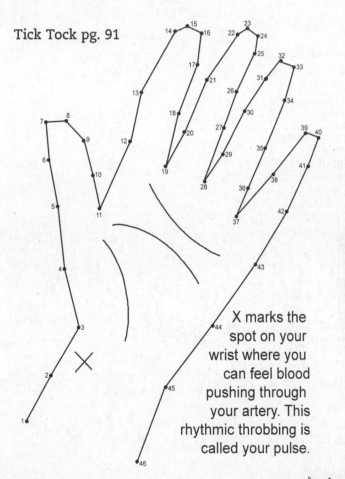

X marks the spot on your wrist where you can feel blood pushing through your artery. This rhythmic throbbing is called your pulse.

Making Music pg. 102

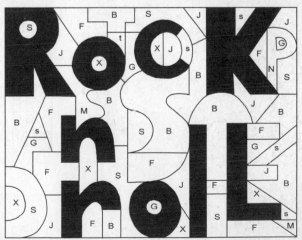

Sweet Lightning pg. 108

Go into a DARK (1) ROOM (2). Look in a MIRROR (3) while you CRUNCH (4) several WINT (5) - O (6) - GREEN (7) LIFE (8) SAVERS (9) in your MOUTH (10). Be sure to CHEW (11) with your MOUTH (10) OPEN (12).

When you chomp the candy, sparks are caused by breaking the sugar molecules. Positive and negative electrical charges make electrons jump between the pieces. While most sugar candies do this, the flash of light is very faint. It is the wintergreen flavouring that helps make a spark you can see.

The Answer pg. 118

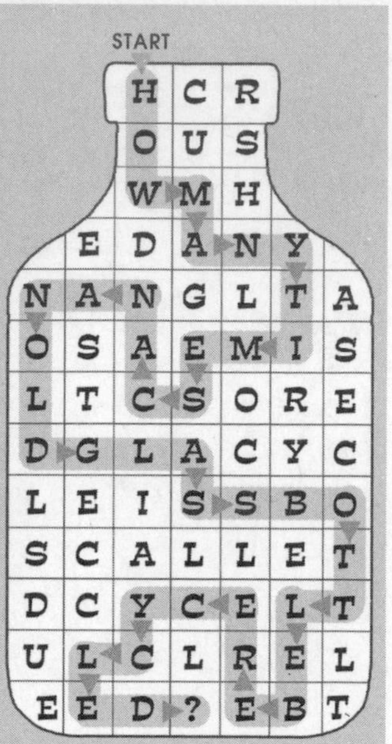

EXTRA LETTERS READ: CRUSHED GLASS TO BE RECYCLED IS CALLED CULLET

Rain in a Jar pg. 105

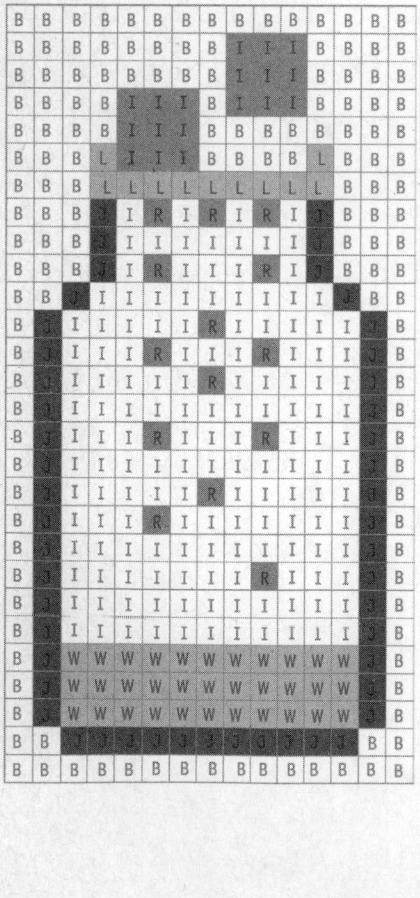

Whole World pg. 112

THIS COMMON BREAKFAST FOOD COMES FROM A CHICKEN AND IS COOKED IN BOILING WATER

The answer to this riddle is a hard-boiled egg! Crack a hard-boiled egg and, without peeling, squeeze it gently. See how the shell buckles in some places? The same type of cracking and moving happens on Earth — we call them earthquakes!

Change of Habit pg. 126

FOR ONE MONTH, HANG
1/3 1/4 1/3 1/2 2/3 1/3 1/2 2/4 2/5 2/5 1/2

CLOTHES OUTSIDE TO DRY.
3/6 2/6 1/3 2/4 2/5 2/3 1/3 2/4 2/3 2/4 1/3 1/4

CHECK THE ELECTRIC BILL
3/6 2/5 2/3 2/4 2/3 2/3 2/6 2/3 3/6 2/4 1/4 3/6 2/6 2/6

BEFORE AND AFTER.
2/3 1/3 1/4 2/3 1/2 2/4 2/3 1/4